Penguin Education

Penguin Papers in Education

Speech and the Development of
Mental Processes in the Child

A. R. Luria and F. Ia. Yudovich

Speech and the Development of Mental Processes in the Child

An experimental investigation by
A. R. Luria and F. Ia. Yudovich,
edited by Joan Simon,
and with a new introduction by James Britton

Penguin Education

Penguin Education, Penguin Books Ltd,
Harmondsworth, Middlesex, England
Penguin Books Inc., 7110 Ambassador Road,
Baltimore, Md 21207, USA
Penguin Books Australia Ltd, Ringwood,
Victoria, Australia
Penguin Books Canada Ltd, 41 Steelcase Road West,
Markham, Ontario, Canada
Penguin Books (N.Z.) Ltd, 182–190 Wairau Road,
Auckland 10, New Zealand

First published in the USSR 1956
This translation first published in Great Britain by
Staples Press 1959
Published in Penguin Books 1971
Reprinted 1972, 1973, 1975
This translation copyright © Staples Press, 1959

Made and printed in Great Britain by
C. Nicholls & Company Ltd
Set in Monotype Times

Contents

Introduction

From many diverse sources has come the idea, the hypothesis, that the importance of language to mankind lies not so much in the fact that it is the means by which we cooperate and communicate with each other as in the fact that it enables each of us, as individuals and in cooperation, to represent the world to ourselves as we encounter it: and so to construct – moment by moment and year after year – a cumulative representation of 'the world as I have known it'. In infancy the representation is made in talk; as for example this four year old who represents to herself, at the moment of encounter, the objects and events that engage her as she plays with her toy farm – to which had recently been added some model zoo animals:

I'm going to have a zoo field . . . now we've got more animals . . . three more, so I think we'll have a zoo field. (*Whispering*) Well, now, let's see . . . let's see how it *feels*. . . . Get this pin now – there, you see. Haven't got a cage . . . should be a zoo man as well. . . . Look, must get this zoo man, then we'll be all right. Really a farm man, but he can be a zoo man. . . . Depends what their job is, doesn't it, Dad? (*She goes off and fetches him.*) There now, you see. . . . What do you want. . . . Well, if you could look after these two elephants . . . I'll go and see about this . . . this panda. Well, all right. He squeezed out, and he got in. Shut the gate again. . . . He said Hello. . . . He said Hello. Dad, what I want to know is if the bear sitting up and the mother can fit in the house. . . . Spect she can though. . . .

The bear . . . Dad, I'm going to call the fellow Brumas, the polar bear fellow. Look, the man and the lady are talking. The man's looking after the elephant and the lady's looking after the polar bear. They're talking over the wall. . . . You didn't see any polar bears, did you?

When a person's standing it's taller than when it's sitting . . . when an animal's sitting it's taller than when it's standing. Spect it's because they've four legs. It's because of the legs . . . your legs go up on the ground, don't they? But really an animal's front paws is really its hands, isn't it? When he sits up (*i.e. the polar bear*) he's as tall as the lady. . . .

Her chatter constitutes a verbal representation of the things she sees and the things that happen – in this case mainly the events she causes to happen. Some of the more general formulations may be important elements in her cumulative representation of the world (as for example her conception of 'home' in the final comment quoted): all may be seen as facilitations at some level of subsequent encounters. On one occasion over a year earlier, when she turned reluctantly from her engrossment with that same toy farm, she said: 'Oh why am I *real* so I can't live in my little farm?' – a representation that surely would persist and evolve through the years.

We continue of course to use talk as a means of representing the world: and that would serve to describe a great deal of the chat and the gossip that most of us devote our time to so generously. But we use writing also, and we use thought – going over in our minds events of the day, for example – and those two processes would not normally be possible to us unless we had built their foundations in speech.

I have arrived at this point, as many others have done, from a desire to understand the nature of language and how it works for us. What I have now to go on to – or back to – is a realization that language is only one of a number of means by which we represent the world to ourselves; furthermore, that what makes us unique among the animals is not our ability to speak *per se*, but our habit of representing experience to ourselves by one means or another. We do so in terms of our own movements, in terms of our perceptions, and probably, more fundamentally still, in terms of our feelings and value-judgements, though this remains a speculation and a mystery; and we do so in language.

We have no difficulty in recognizing the distinction between the process of looking at a face and the process of calling that face to mind, nor in realizing that the two are in some way related. Our ability to call the face to mind is what allows me to talk about a *representation* of the world in terms of perception; the effects of my looking have not been utterly lost when I close my eyes or go away; what I have perceived I have 'represented to myself', and I may go back to the representation long after the face has disappeared from the range of my looking.

Being a man of parts, I can play 'God Save the Queen' on any ordinary piano on request (though three parts of me still wants to call it 'God Save the King'). If, however, you asked me to play the chords that accompany, say 'send her victorious', I should not be able to do so without actually playing, or rehearsing in mind and muscles, the phrases of the tune that lead up to it. I *have* the representation – the fact that I succeed in doing as you ask me would prove that; but it is a representation largely in terms of my movements (in relation to my perception of the piano-keys) and only minimally in terms of the appearance of the notation on the page. Hence I need to go through the repertoire of movements in order to recapture it.

Piaget and Bruner have shown that young children represent the world to themselves first in terms of perception-cum-movement – and I put it that way to indicate that the two are inseparable; and later also in terms of visual imagery, or in perception freed from movement; and that the *simultaneity* of visual representation compared with the *serial* nature of perception-cum-movement results in a better organized system of representing, a more effective filing system for experience.

These two modes of representation are well established before the third, the linguistic mode, comes into operation. When, at about two years of age, a child begins to speak, so achieving this third system, his talk is used as a means of assisting the modes of representation previously acquired; that is to say, the modes of movement and of perception. In fact his language is at first tied to the 'here and now', limited (with a few notable exceptions) to speech about what may be seen and handled in the immediate situation. It is speech-cum-action, or as Luria calls it, 'synpraxic speech' (see page 50). Its function as such is to facilitate activity in the here and now, activity in terms of movement and perception. Parts of the monologue of the four year old quoted above will serve to illustrate this earlier stage. ('Well, if you could look after these two elephants ... I'll go and see about this ... this panda. Well, all right. He squeezed out, and he got in. Shut the gate again ...' etc.) As we read it with imaginative insight I believe we can sense the fact that her speech operates as a way of assisting her moves in the game.

But at one particular point in that monologue we find language operating differently. She talks of things she *wants*, things that are *not* there in front of her – first 'the cage', and then 'the zoo man'; and having spoken of him, off she goes to get him.

This indicates what really amounts to a fourth kind of representation. Just as movement-cum-perception provided the basis from which the second stage was reached, that of perception freed from movement, so language tied to the here-and-now forms the basis from which there develops linguistic representation freed from these bonds, freed from its dependence upon movement and perception. At this fourth stage words come to be used not *with* objects but *in place of them*. As our example directly suggests, the ability to use words in this way further assists exploratory activity by breaking out of the immediate situation. Things previously experienced may be imported into the situation, as the zoo man is: ideas derived from past experience may be brought to bear upon present problems. The result is a wide extension of a child's activities, the enrichment of the possibilities of the here-and-now by drawing upon the resources of the 'not-here' and the 'not-now'.

We are not concerned here simply with what the use of language may import into a situation: we are concerned also with *the way language does so*. Luria has demonstrated in a number of experiments (carried out both before and after the original publication of this book) that what is formulated in language carries a special power to influence a young child's behaviour; that from obeying the verbal instructions of an adult he goes on to instruct himself in words. both directly and indirectly; and that for him *to say what he plans to do* increases his ability to persist and complete an undertaking: that language, in short, performs a *regulative function*.

It has long seemed to me that the great importance of Luria's work in this book lies in its indication of the close relation between language ability and the scope and complexity of human behaviour in general. Of the two outcomes his experiment will report – the effect of encouraging normal speech performance in both the twins, and the further effect of speech training upon one of them – it is the former, the changes of behaviour in both boys after their speech had become 'normal', that is without doubt the major effect. By the same token, Luria's hypothesis that language acquires a regulative function, a power of coordinating, stabilizing and facilitating other forms of behaviour – and the evidence and explanations with which he supports it – form one of the most important contributions he makes in this book to a general reader's understanding of the way language works. His chapter 6 is for this reason a key chapter, and his formulation on page 84 has acquired, in my copy, a kind of illuminated border more often associated with 'texts' of another kind:

With the appearance of speech disconnected from action ... it was to be expected that there should also arise the *possibility of formulating a system of connections transcending the boundaries of the immediate situation* and *of subordinating action to these verbally formulated connections*.

That, taken at its very simplest level, is how the zoo man got to the four year old's model zoo field.

That same four year old had a sister two years younger than herself. One Saturday morning, when they were respectively four and a half and two and a half, I tried, for about fifteen minutes, to keep a record of all that happened and everything they said. During the course of it the older child, Clare, sat on the sofa with coloured pencils and a drawing block and, in spite of interruptions from Alison, the younger child, she completed two pictures; one of a girl riding a pony and one of a girl diving into a pool – both of them references back to things she had seen and done on her summer holiday three months earlier. She talked to herself from time to time about what she was doing ('Want to make your tail a bit shorter – that's what you're wanting.') – but sometimes inaudibly.

Meanwhile, Alison

1. Pretended she was a goat and tried to butt Clare.
2. Tried to climb on to the sofa.
3. Came over to me and claimed my pen.
4. Saw a ruler on the table, asked what it was, wanted it.
5. Crawled under the table.
6. Came out and asked me what I was doing.
7. Climbed on to a chair by the window, looked out and made 'fizzing' noises.
8. Climbed down, saw her shoe on the floor and began to take the lace out.
9. Came over and asked me to put the shoe on her foot.
10. Saw the other shoe, and did the same with that.
11. Went over to Clare and pretended to be a goat again.
12. Climbed on to the sofa and claimed the pencil Clare was using.

It will be clear I think that Alison's behaviour arises almost entirely in response to the various stimuli of the here and now, and is in this respect in direct contrast to Clare's sustained activity. A principal conclusion from Luria's experiment would be that language is the primary means by which the behaviour typical of the four and a half year old is derived from that typical of the two and a half year old – a gain which might crudely be called one of 'undistractability'. The story Luria will tell of the twins in his experiment may in fact be seen as an accelerated journey between the stages represented respectively by Alison and Clare. For those of us who from observation and experience know more about children than we do about psychology, that starting-point may prove a helpful approach to what Luria has to say.

As a child acquires the ability to use language to refer to things not present, it becomes possible for him to represent in words 'what might be' rather than simply 'what is'. As he does so his formulation may equally be a *fiction* – a make-believe – or a *plan*, and sometimes the two will be indistinguishable. A two-year-old child is able to make the first moves in this direction: but the ability either to sustain the make-believe or to carry out the planned activity is one that is developed as the facility in verbalizing grows.

The habit of verbalizing originates in and is fostered above all by speech with an adult: the appropriateness of the adult's early 'instructions' to the child's own concerns, and the eagerness and confidence with which he 'obeys' them, constitute the criteria of favourable conditions. As Luria reminds us (in Vigotsky's words) 'a function which is earlier divided between two people becomes later the means of organization of the child's own behaviour' (page 26).

All that – and I must leave it at that – is the background against which I see Professor Luria's experiment in this book. What I must not do is suggest that it is the background against which the author himself sees it; this he has set out rigorously and fully in his first chapter. (But it is a difficult statement for readers not acquainted with the kind of psychological theories he discusses: I recommend for such readers that they begin reading at chapter 2, taking on trust that first paragraph on page 34, and returning to read chapter 1 when they have read the rest of the book.)

I have discussed *Speech and the Development of Mental Processes in the Child* with a great many teachers and students since the time the English translation was first published in 1959. It has rarely failed, in my experience, to make a strong impact; and its importance has seemed to grow rather than decline as the field in which it operates has become more familiar. It is impossible, moreover, to read the book without finding, between the lines, the human concern and sympathies of its authors: hence, among many other reasons, the honour I feel in being allowed to introduce it to a further generation of readers of the English language.

James Britton 1971

Editorial Note

This book was first published by the Academy of Educational Sciences of the RSFSR in 1956. It has been translated by Mr O. Kovasc and Mrs J. Simon but, because of the obvious difficulties of translating research concerned with primitive and defective speech, the text has been checked by the author who has also made minor amendments and additions for this edition.

It should be noted that Russian is an inflected language which resembles Latin and German from the point of view of morphology. The transliterated examples of both children's speech show that phonetical impairment persisted to a considerable extent even at the close of the experiment; elsewhere this must be assumed as it cannot be adequately reproduced in translation.

The system of transliteration adopted is that used by the British Museum; except that, in order to retain forms now widely accepted, 'y' is used to render the Russian vowel 'bl' (according to the American Library of Congress system) and also used instead of 'i' at the end of proper names. Occasionally softened pronunciation is indicated additionally (e.g. by 'ie' instead of 'e') to bring out mispronunciation more clearly. Finally, though previous translations have rendered the Russian terms 'psikhika' and 'psikhicheskii' as 'psyche' and 'psychic', here 'mind' and 'mental' are used in accordance with the author's advice.

It must be remembered that the pre-school child in the USSR is under seven, the age at which ordinary schooling begins.

Professor Luria heads a group of psychologists at the Institute of Defectology of the Academy of Educational Sciences and is also on the staff of the Department of Psychology, Moscow University. An account of the background of his work, and translations of some of the papers mentioned in this volume, may be found in *Psychology in the Soviet Union*, edited by Brian Simon.

Joan Simon October 1958

Preface to the English Edition

I am very grateful to Mrs Joan Simon for her initiative in arranging the translation of this little book. This enables me to share with English readers observations which were undertaken in collaboration with F. Ia Yudovich many years ago but have only recently been prepared for the press and published.

If an author has the right to express feelings about his own work, I must note the warm sense with which I always turn to the material published in this small book.

The role played by speech in that formation of the child's mental processes is one of the most important psychological questions, but, as is well known, it is very difficult to analyse. Because speech develops in the course of the child's general maturation and development it has seemed almost impossible to assess the specific influence exercised by the child's speech on the development of his mental processes. We must, therefore, particularly value those rare occasions when special conditions enable us to single out the speech factor and, with the aid of an educational experiment, to study its isolated influence.

The investigation of a pair of identical twins with retarded speech and backward behaviour, and of the changes in speech and behaviour brought about by an educational experiment – all of which are described in this book – furnishes material of much interest to psychology, and I am very glad to be able to share the results of this investigation with English readers.

I have long since lost sight of the two twins, Liosha and Yura, but I have preserved over many years the clearest impressions of the work undertaken with them.

A. R. Luria Moscow, February 1958

Preface to the Penguin Edition

I am very glad to learn that my book will appear in the Penguin Papers in Education series.

It is clear that the problems of speech development in children are of the highest importance both for psychology, linguistics and education. A pair of identical twins with retarded speech, who were permanently in each other's company, gave me a wonderful opportunity to study closely the mechanics of speech development and particularly the transition from primitive 'synpraxic' speech to a fully developed form of speech which uses 'syntactic' language. The twins were separated, thus creating the necessity for them to develop conventional language forms and providing me with the opportunity of observing the development of new and higher forms of speech and the more sophisticated forms of behaviour which are closely dependent on language skills.

I can only hope English readers will appreciate the fascination of this process, what new, exciting perspectives in behaviour are evoked by the mastering of language, and how important for a psychologist or a teacher it is to find new ways of analysing it.

A. R. Luria Moscow, August 1971

Chapter 1
The Role of Speech in the Formation of Mental Processes: An Outline of the Problem

The role played by speech in the formation of the child's mental processes was not, for a long period, regarded as an important aspect of psychology.

In studying the development of mental processes, and in the attempt to explain the appearance of complex forms of mental activity (voluntary attention, active memorization or active behaviour), psychologists did not consider the genesis of these processes in connection with the child's basic forms of communication with the surrounding world. Failing to find the real roots of these complex forms of mental activity, they either retreated from scientific analysis or else wrote idealistic tracts about their origin. Typical of the retreat from study of the full complexity of the formation of higher mental processes is the work of a number of behaviourists, beginning with that of Thorndike and Watson and ending with the latest investigations of Guthrie, who consider that all the complex forms of the child's activity can be reduced to a combination of habits, and regard speech itself as an aspect of motor habits which does not have any special place in the child's behaviour.

Typical of the idealistic approach to the origin of complex mental processes is the work of such authors as K. Bühler and Ch. Bühler, who regard the development of the child's higher nervous activity as the gradual unfolding of inborn spiritual qualities, as a simple manifestation of a continuously growing spiritual activity which appears minimally in the early stages of the child's development and, in the process of maturation, gradually begins to take a more and more leading part.

What are the weaknesses of these two standpoints?

To reduce a complex form of the child's mental activity to a combination of elementary motor habits implies a mechanistic approach which ignores what is most essential in man's mental life; which leaves unanswered the question – what special mechanisms differentiate such aspects of activity as voluntary memorization, active attention or volitional activity – though a profound analysis of these mechanisms is one of the basic tasks of educational science.

To regard the development of these forms of mental activity as the simple resultant of maturation of inborn mental properties or abilities is to take up a position already rejected by science; it is to rely, when treating concrete aspects of the formation of an organism's structure and activity, on the influence of some kind of further, unanalysable 'inner force' which is not subject to any kind of formation but only appears, is manifested, in the process of development.

These standpoints are defective not only in theory but also in practice. They imply a departure from scientific investigation of *how* complex forms of activity are gradually constructed in the process of the child's development and his active, living communication with the environment, by regarding them as the mechanical product of training or as the simple maturing of primary 'spiritual qualities'. These conceptions disarm educational science which is fundamentally concerned with the formative influencing of the child's mental development.

The first of these theories, regarding complex development as a combination of simple habits, reduces teaching and education to simple training; the second, regarding 'the maturation of mental abilities' as a spontaneously continuous process, not only shrugs off the problem of explaining the mechanisms of mental development but also relegates educational influences to a very subsidiary place, understanding them at most as a means of speeding up, or slowing down, 'natural maturation', the direction of which is predetermined. In practice, as in theory, this idealistic approach to the development of complex mental processes in man has long since become an obstacle to a scientific understanding of the mind.[1]

Soviet psychology has completely rejected these oversimplified and unscientific conceptions. The theoretical prerequisites of a scientific approach to the development of complex mental activity, the conceptions which inform Soviet psychology, can be expressed in three fundamental propositions.

Materialist psychology rejects as useless the approach to any form of mental activity – and, in particular, the more complex forms – as the product of unanalysable 'abilities' which are innate in the organization of the brain. Proceeding from the reflex theory advanced by Sechenov and elaborated by Pavlov, it regards all mental processes as complex functional formations which are built up as an outcome of concrete forms of interaction between the organism and its environment. In the process of concrete activity, through reflex responses to the environment, dynamic systems or 'systems of functions' are formed which we have no foundation to regard as innate properties of mental life; which can only be understood as the outcome of certain forms of reflex activity subject at every point to concrete analysis.[2]

This first proposition of materialist psychology, which has a firm philosophical basis in Lenin's theory of reflection, makes possible a new kind of approach to all the complex forms of mental life; one which, rejecting all attempts to seek their roots in the 'depths of the soul', turns to real forms of interrelation between organism and environment. This point of departure, which entirely reverses views that have prevailed for centuries, clearly has a decisive significance for the science of psychology.

The second proposition of Soviet psychology, also basic to materialist science, is the introduction of the role of development into study of the formation of mental processes.

Sechenov considered that a scientific psychology must be concerned with the 'formation of mental activity'. From this position he decisively overturned metaphysical conceptions which characterize mental phenomena as the product of eternally existing properties, and emphasized that an approach to these phenomena from the standpoint of development was the essential condition for an embodiment of the reflex theory.

Only a clear understanding that, at each particular stage of development, concrete forms of activity present the organism with new problems, new demands, which necessitate the development of new forms of reflex action, only such a conception can ensure the development of scientific research into the basic laws governing the formation of complex aspects of human mental activity.

This is the direction taken by Soviet psychological research.

The third proposition of Soviet psychology is study of the child's mental activity as the outcome of his life in certain determined social circumstances. Human mental activity takes place in conditions of actual communication with the environment, in the course of which the child acquires from adults the experience of many generations. The transition from the animal world to the stage of man signifies the introduction of a new principle of development. At the animal stage the development of higher nervous processes in each species is the outcome of individual experience but with the transition to man the basic form of mental development becomes acquisition of the experiences of other people through joint practice and speech.

Language, which incorporates the experience of generations or, more broadly speaking, of mankind, is included in the process of the child's development from the first months of his life. By naming objects, and so defining their connections and relations, the adult creates new forms of reflection of reality in the child, incomparably deeper and more complex than those which he could have formed through individual experience. This whole process of the transmission of knowledge and the formation of concepts, which is the basic way the adult influences the child, constitutes the central process of the child's intellectual development. If this formation of the child's mental activity in the process of education is left out of consideration, it is impossible either to understand or to explain causally any of the facts of child psychology.

Study of the child's mental processes as the product of his intercommunication with the environment, as the acquisition of common experiences transmitted by speech, has, therefore, become the most important principle of Soviet psychology which informs all research.

Since this principle has such decisive significance, and since it is central to our investigation, it is necessary to examine this question more fully.

It would be mistaken to suppose that verbal intercourse with adults merely changes the content of the child's conscious activity without changing its form.

Intercommunication with adults is of decisive significance because the acquisition of a language system involves a re-organization of all the child's basic mental processes; the word thus becomes a tremendous factor which forms mental activity, perfecting the reflection of reality and creating new forms of attention, of memory and imagination, of thought and action.

With the acquisition of such an 'extraordinary supplement' as the word, the most important factor emerging at the stage of man, there is introduced, in the words of Pavlov, 'a new principle of nervous activity ... the abstraction and with this the generaliza-tion of the innumerable signals of the preceding system, and, again ... analysis and synthesis of these new generalized signals; on this depends man's infinite capacity for orientation in the environment, and, too, his highest form of adaptation – science'.[3]

The word has a basic function not only because it indicates a corresponding object in the external world, but also because it abstracts, isolates, the necessary signal, generalizes perceived signals and relates them to certain categories; it is this systematiz-ation of direct experience that makes the role of the word in the formation of mental processes so exceptionally important.

The mother's very first words, when she shows her child dif-ferent objects and names them with a certain word, have an in-discernible but decisively important influence on the formation of his mental processes. The word, connected with direct perception of the object, isolates its essential features; to name the perceived object 'a glass', adding its functional role 'for drinking', isolates the essential and inhibits the less essential properties of the object (such as its weight or external shape); to indicate with the word 'glass' any glass, regardless of its shape, makes perception of this object permanent and generalized.

The word, handing on the experience of generations as this

experience is incorporated in language, locks a complex system of connections in the child's cortex and becomes a tremendous tool, introducing forms of analysis and synthesis into the child's perception which he would be unable to develop by himself. For instance, when he acquires the word 'inkstand' (chernilnitsa) the child necessarily acquires also a form of systematization of perceived phenomena. He relates 'inkstand' to the groups of things related to colours (chern-, black), tools (-il-, the suffix for most Russian words designating tools) and containers (-nits-, the suffix for words designating these). As the word influences the child, therefore, it deepens and immeasurably enriches his direct perception, forms his consciousness.

This reorganization of perception – this transference of human consciousness from the stage of direct sensory experience to the stage of generalized, rational understanding – by no means exhausts the influence of the word in the formation of mental processes.

When he acquires a word, which isolates a particular thing and serves as a signal to a particular action, the child, as he carries out an adult's verbal instruction, is subordinated to this word. The adult's word becomes a regulator of his behaviour and the organization of the child's activity is thereby lifted to a higher, qualitatively new, stage. This subordination of his reactions to the word of an adult is the beginning of a long chain of formation of complex aspects of his conscious and voluntary activity.

By subordinating himself to the adult's verbal orders the child acquires a system of these verbal instructions and gradually begins to utilize them for the regulation of his own behaviour. Repeating the verbal indication of an object, he places it amongst other directly perceived things and makes it the object of his own complex active attention. When he establishes verbally the complex connections and relations between perceived phenomena he introduces essential changes in the perception of things influencing him; he begins to act according to verbally elaborated influences by reproducing the verbal connections reinforced by earlier adult instructions, and thereafter modifies them, isolating verbally the immediate and final aims of his behaviour, indicating the means of achieving these aims and subordinating these aims to verbally formulated instructions. By these means the child advances to the stage of a new form of regulating his behaviour which gradually becomes, in Pavlov's words, 'a system, a unitary, higher form of self-regulation'. In sum, speech, the basic means of communication, becomes also a means of deeper analysis and synthesis of reality and, more fundamentally important, 'a higher regulator of behaviour'.

All this has a decisive significance for materialist psychology. The fact that the word is included in the content of nearly all basic forms of human activity, that it participates in the formation of perception and memory, in stimulus and action, permits a new approach to an important region of mental activity. Perception and attention, memory and imagination, consciousness and action, cease to be regarded as simple, eternal, innate mental 'properties'. They begin to be understood as the product of complex social forms of the child's mental processes; as complex 'systems of functions' which appear as a result of the development of the child's activity in the process of intercourse; as complex reflective acts in the content of which speech is included, which, using Pavlov's terminology, are realized with the close participation of the two signal systems – the first signal system being concerned with directly perceived stimuli, the second with systems of verbal elaboration.

Only by understanding that the sources of all complex mental processes do not lie in the depths of the soul, but are to be found in complex forms of human social life and in the child's communication with people surrounding him, can we finally outgrow the prejudices which have been rooted for centuries in psychological science.

Soviet psychologists began to study the child's mental development in close connection with the development of speech three decades ago and there are a number of works dealing with this question.

L. S. Vigotsky was one of the first to express the view that speech plays a decisive role in the formation of mental processes, and that the basic method of analysing the development of higher psychological functions is investigation of that re-organization of mental processes which takes place under the influence of speech.

He investigated the development of understanding in children and reached the conclusion that characteristic forms of com-munication begin when there is generalization of several objects as a whole from direct impressions, and end when each process of analysis and synthesis of reality is defined by a word which dis-tinguishes the necessary features and relates the perceived object to a definite category.[4] Vigotsky and his colleagues undertook a whole series of experimental investigations: into the process of formation of active attention which begins to be built up by the directive participation of the word; into the process of develop-ment of memory which, with the mediation of the word, becomes progressively transformed into active, voluntary memorization;[5] into the development of several other higher mental processes, the analysis of which invariably showed that their complex functional organization was built up with the closest participation of speech.

All these researches convinced Vigotsky of the great signific-ance of speech in the formation of mental processes. Besides investigating the basic stages of development of complex mental processes through the organization of speech, he also arrived at the fundamental conclusion that human mental development has its source in the verbal communication between child and adult, that 'a function which is earlier divided between two people becomes later the means of organization of the child's own behaviour'.

Vigotsky's researches were followed by numerous other studies of the part played by the word as the basis of systems of connec-tions which allow for further formation of the child's mental pro-cesses.

Towards the close of the 1930s and the beginning of the 1940s, G. L. Rosengardt undertook an interesting series of investigations which demonstrated the role of the word in the formation of per-ceptions and in memorization during the first two years of life. This and other similar research[6] showed convincingly not only that the word is gradually excluded from other complexes perceived by the child, but also the decisively important fact that, under its influence, the young child's perception and memory acquire new features; by allowing him to distinguish the essential features of an object the word makes his perception of objects generalized and constant and creates new possibilities for the development of coherent, differentiated memory.

Further research underlined the essential role played by speech in complex forms of child behaviour.[7] The development of active forms of memorization, the earliest forms of the child's volitional behaviour and, in particular, the differentiation of motives of behaviour and the construction of complex conscious actions – all these have proved to be closely connected with those complex reorganizations of activity which appear in the process of generization, and to stand in close relation to the development of the child's speech. Verbal processes, through generalization, enable the child to formulate aims and the necessary means for their achievement, to create an 'imaginative' play plan in subordination to which he can acquire complex forms of behaviour which are inaccessible to a direct attempt. Investigation of the genesis of higher forms of psychological activity once more demonstrated their complex composition and the role of speech in forming the child's consciousness.

Of recent years, Soviet psychologists and physiologists have not limited themselves to these questions but have also described changes in the course of nervous processes as a result of the participation of the second signal system.

A. G. Ivanov-Smolensky and N. I. Krasnogorsky long since attempted to show in practice the role of the word in the child's higher nervous activity.[8] Their researches showed that the word can successfully replace unconditioned reinforcement, that with the aid of constant reinforcement of a conditioned signal through verbal instruction it is possible to form a new temporary connection, as successfully as by use of an unconditioned (food or defensive) reinforcement. Experiments undertaken by Ivanov-Smolensky's students also showed that the word can successfully replace a direct conditioned signal, that the reaction earlier obtained to the picture of a sparrow can easily and at once be obtained by substituting the word 'sparrow', the related word 'swallow', or the generalizing word 'bird'. Several other psychologists obtained similar data.[9]

This work proved that the word can replace unconditioned or conditioned stimuli. Further research has underlined the essential fact that the word exercises a significant influence on the course of elaboration of temporary connections, hastening the process of elaboration, rendering the connections more stable and contributing substantially new features to their formation.

When elaborating differentiation in children of one and a half to two years, A. A. Lublinskaya noted that difficulties in differentiating strongly decreased when verbal labels were added to the differentiating signals. Children undergoing the experiment were able to differentiate four to five times more quickly than children in the control group and the differentiations elaborated with the participation of the word were more stable and generalized than those elaborated without it.[10]

Special research has also shown that the experimenter's instructions not only significantly hasten the process of elaboration of new temporary connections and make them more stable, but also essentially reorganize the natural course of these processes, for instance, by changing the natural relation of the strength of stimuli. It is well known that with the usual complex stimuli the leading role is played by the strong component, while the weak component of the complex retreats into the background and is inhibited by the strong one.[11] But the word of the experimenter (or systems of previous connections evoked by the word) reinforce the weak component of the complex so that it changes into the strong, leading one, while the physically stronger component loses its leading significance.[12]

It is interesting to note that in the usual experimental conditions the word had this effect with four- to five-year-old children, whereas in cases where the word of the experimenter revives stable old connections a change in the strength relations of stimuli occurs much earlier. Even more interesting is the fact that the child's speech itself begins to be progressively included in the formation of temporary connections and essentially changes this process.

Already in 1929 Vigotsky showed that every time the little child of four to five years of age is confronted with a problem which causes some kind of difficulty, there arises external speech, not directed to his interlocutor; the child states the situation that has arisen, takes from it 'verbal copy' and then reproduces those connections of his past experience which may help him out of present difficulties. Vigotsky attempted to show that this was not affective 'egocentric speech', about which Piaget was then writing, but the inclusion of speech to mediate behaviour by the mobilization of verbal connections which help to solve a difficult problem. His observations showed that the child first speaks aloud, to himself, but that his speech gradually dies away, passes into a whisper and finally becomes internal speech; and that the child of seven to eight years begins to solve complex problems with the aid of systems of internal verbal connections, which have arisen earlier in the course of verbal intercourse but have since become converted into his own individual mechanisms, enabling him to include verbal connections in the organization of his activity.[13]

A period of twenty years elapsed before the data obtained by Vigotsky were checked and proved by new research. N. P. Paramonova, analysing the process of formation of motor reactions in the normal pre-school child, showed that the inclusion of his own speech as a means of organizing his activity itself represents a complex and developing process. In the case of the child of three years, the elaboration of temporary connections by the method of verbal reinforcement is not yet mediated by his own speech, which gradually dies away, and proceeds slowly; but with the child of four to five years the process substantially changes. The appearance of the signal, accompanied by reinforcement, first calls forth questions from the child ('Do I have to press on this one?') and afterwards produces positive repetitions ('This red one! I have to press this!'); this shows that the connections elaborated have achieved their generalized verbal formulation.[14]

These verbal repetitions are preserved for some time, but in the six- to seven-year-old child they die away and vanish. What is characteristic here is the fact that, with the appearance of verbal formulations – in other words with inclusion of the child's own speech in his orientation to the signals presented – the very process of elaboration of new connections changes. Connections which were previously elaborated gradually, which needed permanent reinforcement and were extinguished when it was removed, begin now to be elaborated quickly, sometimes 'on the spot', become stably reinforced, cease to be in need of permanent reinforcement and begin to show those features of 'self-regulation' which Pavlov regarded as the essential peculiarity of human higher nervous activity.

The direct participation of the child's own speech in the process of elaboration of new connections is, according to these findings,[15] well established in the child of five to six years. However, other research has shown that this participation of speech in the elaboration of new connections can be essentially disturbed by injuries to the brain and also by abnormal development; above all by that form of mental retardation which results from acute organic disease of the brain in early childhood.[16]

In such cases the processes of higher nervous activity are so imperfect and the very speech of the child so defective – so poor are his connections, so immobile his dynamics – that the participation of speech in the formation of new connections becomes impossible and these are elaborated without the requisite participation of the abstracting and generalizing function of the word. It is precisely because of this that the mentally retarded schoolchild does not show those features of swift, mobile and stable elaboration of new connections which, as has just been pointed out, are characteristic features of the realization of this process when there is full-value participation of the two signal systems. The process of elaborating new connections becomes slow and gradual, continues for a long time to depend on permanent reinforcement, remains stable only because of the strictly determined discipline of the experiment, is easily inhibited by complication of the conditions and is not reflected in any kind of coherent verbal formulation.

Observations of mentally retarded children permit us to approach the problem of the role of speech in the formation of temporary connections from another angle; to study how the child's behaviour differs when the abstraction and generalization of speech plays no part in its formation.[17]

Investigations of mentally retarded children belong to a new region of study where different methods are used to throw light on the role of speech in the formation of complex aspects of mental activity; this research is concerned with the data of psychopathology.

About thirty years ago the German psychopathologist K. Goldstein and his colleague, the psychologist A. Gelb, expressed the view that the acquisition of speech allowed man to rise above direct, visual perception to analysis of its data, to the relation of perceived objects to certain categories, so enabling him to organize his behaviour, not according to the visually perceived situation, but according to a deeper 'categorized' reflection of the world. They therefore connected freer, 'categorized' behaviour with acquisition of the word; very similar views were advanced by the well-known English neurologist, H. Head.

After prolonged research they advanced the hypothesis that this complicated structure of 'abstract' or 'categorized' behaviour, which is a characteristic human feature, falls to pieces in cases of special verbal disorder – aphasia – which arise as a result of disturbances in the normal functioning of the cortex. They connected this disturbance of speech with the patient's return to more primitive and concrete behaviour. In the case of such patients, the possibility of advancing from the direct perceptional field is excluded and what should be an abstract 'categorized' operation becomes a simple reproduction of visual situations well established in the patient's previous experience.[18]

This material provides a valuable illustration of the role of the word in the organization of complex mental processes and indicates the tremendous damage to human behaviour as a result of its loss. Research into the changes in mental processes in states of aphasia has contributed substantially to our understanding of the dependence of complex mental processes on speech; after these investigations it is difficult to deny that many of those higher psychological functions which have so often been discussed as manifestations of innate properties in fact result from the inclusion in activity of that tremendous formative factor, the word.

The data of psychopathological research, accumulated by Gelb, Goldstein, Head and other neurologists abroad, find a clear explanation in the psychology of higher nervous activity; in particular in Pavlov's finding concerning the interaction of the two signal systems and their participation in the formation of every human activity. Closely related data, which permit of an approach to the same question from another angle, have been obtained by psychologists who have investigated the peculiarities of mental processes in deaf-mutes.

The time has long since passed when the deaf-mute child was regarded as differing from his normal counterpart only by the absence of hearing and speech. Research carried out abroad, and by Soviet psychologists, has shown the changes that take place in the deaf-mute's perceptual processes because of his undeveloped speech; excluded from speech communication because of his defect in hearing, he does not possess all those forms of reflection of reality which are realized through verbal speech. The deaf-mute who has not been taught to speak indicates objects or actions with a gesture; he is unable to abstract the quality or action from the actual object, to form abstract concepts, to systematize the phenomena of the external world with the aid of the abstracted signals furnished by language but which are not natural to visual, practically acquired experience. The psychological research of Vigotsky and others[19] and the educational observations of teachers of deaf-mutes show how great a degree of underdevelopment of complex perceptual processes accompanies all deaf-muteness, and how much effort must be spent to restore these serious defects in complex psychological processes by continuous teaching of verbal speech.

All this rich and many-sided research contributes important material towards elucidation of the part played by speech in the formation of the child's mental activity and lays a sound foundation for further studies of this kind. Nevertheless, this research has come up against several practical difficulties to which we may now turn.

Chapter 2
Methods of Studying the Role of Speech in the Formation of Mental Processes

The research already described proves that speech plays a vital part in the organization of complex forms of mental activity. But this does not mean that detailed study of the connections between speech and general mental development is easy. The task of studying these interrelations in specific conditions gives rise to several substantial difficulties and we must, therefore, turn aside to discuss the methods that can best encompass this study while at the same time fully complying with the requirements of exact science.

Three methods are generally used for study of the participation of speech in the formation of mental processes. First, there are investigations of the child's mental development which concentrate on variations in the construction of his activity in the course of the development of his speech. Secondly, research is concerned with cases in which injuries to the brain have led to the disintegration of speech; analysis of changes in the mental processes of such patients gives rise to conclusions about the role of speech in the course of normal mental development. Thirdly, a special experimental method is used which involves either the inclusion of speech in the fulfilment of various tasks or its exclusion from their fulfilment.

When investigating the variations that occur in the child's mental processes with the development of his speech, we cannot in practice separate two closely connected factors: the variation in the organization of mental processes which is connected with maturation and that which depends on the changing forms of the child's life activity as a whole, the changes in his conditions of life. These two factors overlap the development of his speech so closely that it is practically impossible to separate one from the other.

It is quite natural, then, that research workers who have utilized this method have often erroneously attributed to the development of speech changes which were in fact the result of more complex factors in the development of the child's activity as a whole. Therefore, though a significant number of the investigations referred to above show clearly the dependence of mental processes on the development of speech, they have not given a sufficiently precise answer to the question – which variations in these processes are connected with the inclusion of speech and which are the resultant of general variations in the child's activity connected with maturation and with changes in his conditions of life?

The second method, that of analysing variations in cases of brain injury which produce disintegration of speech, is not so precise as it seems at first glance. Brain injuries cause deep disturbances in the dynamics of nervous processes which are characteristic of the normal functioning of the brain. This is necessarily directly reflected in the dynamics of several higher cortical functions and so indirectly reflected in speech activity. It is difficult to verify which variations in mental processes are the result of disturbances in the functioning of the brain as a whole and which are the specific consequence of disturbances of speech.

Many psychological investigations of aphasia have not, therefore, provided quite convincing conclusions about the dependence of various aspects of mental activity on speech. Utilization of this method of research is further complicated by the fact that the disintegration of speech which results from local injuries to the brain is seldom complete. Several investigations have shown that injury to the brain can lead directly to disturbance of one or another of the analysers,* thus calling forth disturbances of different aspects

*The term 'analyser' was introduced by Pavlov, in place of the designation 'sense organ', to denote the whole analysing apparatus of the nervous system; e.g. the acoustic (or visual etc.) analyser covers not only the peripheral receptor with all its afferent nerves but also the nerve cells which lie at the central termination of the nerve fibres, in the cortex, and must each be related to some definite element of some definite form of energy. Pavlov also regarded the motor region of the cortex as an analyser of impulses from the muscles and joints. [Ed.]

of the complex act of speech but not leading every time to the same disturbances of mental processes.

The investigation of cases involving local injury to the brain does not, therefore, allow us adequately to assess the role played by speech in the formation of normal mental activity. This method of objective study suffers from several deficiencies and can only be accepted with essential reservations.

Even greater difficulties attend the third method, that of experimental inclusion of speech in the accomplishment of various tasks or experimental exclusion of speech from the process under investigation. Research workers have attempted artificially to exclude the participation of speech from mental activity by various means in order to study which processes are disturbed by its exclusion.[20] But the operation of the law of elective irradiation in the brain means that internal speech participates intimately in nearly all forms of human mental activity and the attempt to exclude it does not usually result in more than a partial limitation of this participation; therefore only in exceptional cases can this method be utilized with any degree of success.[21]

The best way of avoiding these fundamental problems is to investigate cases of retardation in the development of the child's speech processes; in such cases an artificially hastened acquisition of speech may lead not only to enrichment of speech activity but also to a substantial reorganization of the child's whole mental development.

An investigation of this kind eliminates the factors of gradual maturation and pathological variation in the dynamics of nervous processes which seriously complicate research. If the child's speech activity can be changed in a relatively short time it becomes possible to investigate variations in mental processes which arise as a direct consequence of this development of speech.

Again, cases of retarded speech development are most profitable because this occurs not so much as a result of organic causes (such as innate underdevelopment of the speech apparatus) but rather because the child's situation has not evoked an urgent necessity for the development of speech communication. By changing the given situation and so creating an objective necessity for speech communication we can call forth a rapid development of the child's speech and then investigate how this effects changes in the structure of mental processes.

Cases of retarded speech development in twins growing up together are obviously the most suitable for investigation. It has long since been noted that there is a certain tendency to retardation of speech when twins grow up together. Since their lives are linked in the closest way, and they understand each other in the course of joint practical activity, twins are not faced with an objective necessity for transition to speech communication so frequently as other children. If to this factor is added another which inhibits timely development of speech (for instance, retarded development of the speech motor analyser) then sharply delineated defects in speech communication may be observed even in children of four to five years.

Such cases are, then, particularly favourable for our purposes. Speech retardation implies that a child who is relatively mature in his physical development does not possess a developed speech system. The peculiar way of life paired together with a brother (the 'twin situation'), which does not create any pressing, objective necessity for speech communication, fixes this retardation. Consequently there must also be underdevelopment of all those aspects of mental activity which depend on the acquisition of full-value speech.

Cases of this kind have various advantages from the point of view of research. The retardation in speech can be corrected relatively easily and quickly. If the twins are separated for some time and placed in a normal situation of communication with speaking children, one of the factors reinforcing the underdevelopment of speech is removed and there is created an objective necessity for speech development, as the most important means of communication which is completely accessible to their age.

Comparatively little work with sound and sound-articulating analysis will be sufficient to overcome defects due to the late development of differentiated phonematic hearing, one of the main factors delaying the formation of speech at an early age.

Because of the relatively rapid acquisition of speech the result-ant peculiarities in the development of mental processes would be the product of the one changed factor – the acquisition of a system of language and speech communication – rather than the result of gradual maturation.

Consequently an educational experiment of this kind could contribute to the solution of that most important psychological problem, the role of speech in the formation of mental processes.

We were able to undertake such an experiment. We observed over a considerable period two twins of five years old, similar in genetic constitution (that is, uniovular twins), who as a result of retarded speech development were not possessed of developed, grammatical speech. We were able to remove the factor retarding the development of speech, the 'twin situation', by separating them for three months and placing them in parallel groups in a kindergarten. Finally we were able to teach one of them, develop-ing in him correct, grammatical speech.

In the course of this experiment we were able to observe that reorganization of the child's whole mental activity which is brought about by speech, while specifically distinguishing sup-plementary variations which arose as a result of the specially planned teaching of speech.

Chapter 3
The Twins G:
Psychological Characteristics

Our subjects were two uniovular twins, Yura and Liosha G, who exhibited complex phonetical impairment and, at a comparatively late age, retarded, primitive speech – so-called 'autonomous speech.*

The twin brothers were the last children of a large family. There were five other children, ranging from nine to twenty-two years, all of whom were healthy and had developed well. We traced back late development of speech and compensatory speech defects in the mother's line; the mother and her brother only began to speak well at eight years and even now suffer from the remnants of complex phonetical impairment. Both twins were born at the normal term and, with the exception of their retarded speech, their early development was normal. Neither of them displayed any signs of mental retardation; their sole defect consisted in a very considerable retardation in their speech development.

The twins did not speak at all up to the age of two years; at the age of two and a half they had only learned to say 'mama' and 'papa'; at four years their speech consisted only in a small number of barely differentiated sounds which they used in play and communication. At this stage their mother was unable to note any stable words applied to any object or action. At the age of five the twins' speech consisted of a small number of customary words (often very distorted) and a few 'autonomous' words and sounds; the words of common speech were used mainly in communication with adults and mostly in the form of replies to questions. In communication with each other the twins' speech consisted of sounds and separate words, inextricably connected

*Under 'autonomous' speech (a designation introduced by Eliasberg and other German psychologists) we understand speech which does not possess the developed system of normal language.

with direct actions and accompanied by lively gesticulation. Their speech activity as a whole was very small and often during half an hour of play they pronounced only a few words and sounds. Usually this 'autonomous' speech was inhibited or ceased on the appearance of an adult and only when the observer was not noticed was it possible to hear during their play such sounds as: 'aga', 'ni', 'ntsa', 'en', 'a', 'bul-bul' etc. On an equal footing with these was repetition of their own names 'Liosia' (Liosha) and 'Liulia' (Yura). Sometimes general sounds were heard imitating the words of 'autonomous' speech; 'pi-pi' for chicken, 'kva' for frog etc. A small stock of normal words comprised names of domestic objects, parts of the body, a few animals and birds and elementary actions. The twins' speech was phonetically impaired, many sounds were not pronounced at all, many that should have been voiced were pronounced as softened.

The twins' understanding of other people's speech was obviously unsatisfactory. They understood usual, everyday speech when it directly referred to them but their comprehension of grammatically more complex speech which was not accompanied by explanatory actions was altogether imperfect. Speech which did not directly refer to them usually completely passed them by.

At home the twins spent most of their time in play with each other; there was nothing organized to keep them occupied and they were usually left on their own. They never heard a book read, nor were they told stories, and they only listened to strangers talking if they heard their own names mentioned.

In spite of all this, the twins did not give the impression of being mentally retarded. They were good, cheerful, energetic, mischievous, friendly and affectionate; their movements were sufficiently alert and rhythmic and they displayed musicality. Both were efficient during meals and with their clothes, serving themselves and refusing help. When they were placed together in the kindergarten* they willingly participated in duties, quickly orientated themselves in the new setting and did not present any difficulties to the teacher.

*A residential kindergarten where the children stay all the weekdays. [Ed.]

Further observations brought to light several peculiarities in their behaviour as compared with other children of the same age.

The content of their play was always very primitive and monotonous and led to the manipulation of objects independently of any other aspect of the play materials provided. Not once was there observed any tendency to the simplest construction with building materials; cubes were only piled up or laid in a row on the ground. They liked large building materials but their play with these consisted only in transporting them from one corner to another without any attempt to use them for building. Play of a creative, meaningful character was rare and extremely monotonous, being repeated without variations. Such games as lotto did not attract their attention at all.

The twins seldom played with the other children and only occasionally took part in mobile games with simple actions, such as chasing and catching and 'train' which do not require strict division of roles nor unification of the separate elements of play in a general imaginative whole; they never took part in complex, meaningful play nor in such creative activities as modelling, drawing etc. Only after several months did they produce their first 'drawing', a few greasy marks with paint which obviously did not correspond to their age.

During most of the initial period in the kindergarten they did not choose to have permanent communication with any of the other children but usually passed their time in each other's company. It was often observed that when another child cried they at first listened with alarm, but becoming convinced that the cry came from some irrelevant child they at once relaxed, as much as to say 'Not Liosia', 'Not Liulia'. Without each other they were restless and if one was absent the other looked for him. If one was punished, the other also cried, but if any other child was punished they did not usually react.

In spite of the great similarity between the twins there were also significant differences. Liosha (Twin B in the experiment) weighed six pounds at birth, took to the breast at once and had never been ill. Yura (Twin A in the experiment) weighed three and three-quarter pounds at birth, was very weak, had to be kept warm by artificial means for two months after birth and at five months suffered from influenza with a high temperature; he began to sit later, to walk one and a half months later and was teething later than Liosha. The mother remarked that Liosha was more active and that Yura was subordinated by him. Nevertheless, as will be indicated below, the twins' speech development was at first observed to be very similar.

Chapter 4
Peculiarities in the Structure and Function of Speech in the Twins G

The initial period during which we observed the twins was in some respects a transitional one. With the acquisition to their vocabulary of several commonly used words their speech became more normal, but in its structural and functional peculiarities it remained wholly primitive 'autonomous' speech. The twins G had not yet been separated and played closely together, having very little to do with the others; they usually passed their time in primitive play or occupied with simple stereotyped repetition of manipulations of objects. We were unable to register any speech initiated by them with adults. Communication with adults was limited to this; one or both of the twins approached the teacher and pointed to some object which had attracted their attention. Their unwillingness to follow the teacher's suggestions was most often expressed by actions or a cry. Attempts to draw them into conversation usually met with silence, though sometimes in reply to a direct question they pointed at the thing mentioned. It was in such a situation that the twins most often used the common word, hardly phonetically distorted; less often there slipped in some 'autonomous' expression denoting the given object.

Their speech in communication with each other was built up in an entirely different way. Here it was observed that it most often accompanied their play and activities, it expressed their wishes and invited the partner to some kind of action. In this 'play' situation the words of common speech were more seldom used and 'autonomous' words, sharply differing from the common ones, were chiefly employed.

We may now look at the lexicology and semantics, the grammar and function of the twins' speech during the first stage of our observations.

Lexicology and semantics of the 'autonomous' speech of twins G

In order to analyse the lexicological composition of the speech of the twins G, we registered (by keeping a continuous record) everything that they pronounced in the course of communication with each other, and the answers they gave to adult questions, during a period of some two to three weeks.

As is shown in Table 1, the words of common speech, though they were defectively pronounced,* constituted 54·3 per cent of their whole vocabulary; 34 per cent of their speech consisted of distorted words in which it was often difficult to recognize the words of common speech.†

A considerably smaller proportion, 11·7 per cent, consisted of 'autonomous' words proper, in the number of which were included expressions of the type 'ntsa' (yes, so, all right, quickly – indications of pleasure), 'aga' (so, well done, good), 'toutou' (car, to go etc.), 'fouou' (a bear, terrible), 'maliaka' (bad), 'otop-top' (high, many).

Table 1 Analysis of Vocabulary of Twins G
(Active and Answered Speech)

Types of word in the speech of Twins G	Number of words	%
Common words of narrative speech	74	54·3
Distorted words (with special meaning)	46	34·0
Autonomous words (sounds, imitations etc.)	16	11·7
Total	136	100·0

This might give the impression that words differing from those of common speech composed an insignificant proportion of the

*For example 'otki' for ochki (spectacles); 'tym' for dym (smoke); 'tol' for stol (table) etc.

†For example 'pas' for spat (to sleep); 'a-ma' for slomàl (I broke); 'sìsi' for kìsa (a cat).

twins' language; that this did not differ notably from the common speech of a normal child and so had no special psychological interest.

But closer analysis shows that, though the formal lexicological composition of the twins' speech seems to approach that of common speech, significant peculiarities appear when the words are classified according to their meaning and use.

The first fact to be noted is the *imprecisely* expressed generalization, the *diffusion* of meaning of the words in our twins' language.

Very often the same objects were indicated by different words, either common or autonomous; for instance, sobàka (a dog) by 'abàka', 'abbà'; mishka (a bear) by 'fou-ou', 'mitka'; lòshadka (a horse) by 'liasadka', 'tplu-tplu'.

On the other hand, each word did not always have a stable, precise meaning but was used to refer to a whole group of objects and actions. Sometimes it obviously had a generalized objective meaning; it was clear that the twins expressed by a word some common feature which they had distinguished in several related object groups. For instance, the word 'ìtik' (lìstik, a leaf) indicated both a leaf and a flower; the word 'makòka' (morkòvka, a carrot) indicated a carrot, a turnip, a water-melon, a plum etc. Often the words indicated objects, actions and quality at the same time: 'amà' (slomàl, I broke) signified I broke and also a hurt spot, a tear etc.; 'pipis' (pit-pit, to drink) indicated a teapot, a cup, to drink and water. Finally some words, for instance 'ntsa', 'aga', 'op' only had meaning in dependence upon the situation in which they were included.

Our observations showed, therefore, that even the words of common speech were used by the twins with a very generalized, diffuse meaning, often indicating an object and also an action and quality. Clearly this kind of speech evinced peculiarities proper to a considerably earlier phase of speech development, such as are usually observed in children towards the end of the second and the beginning of the third year of life.

It is particularly noteworthy that in many cases the words used by our twins did not have a stable meaning and only acquired meaning by entering into some operative situation.

At first glance it may seem that words which did not possess permanent, stable meanings were exceptions which consituted only an insignificant proportion of the twins' speech. However, detailed analysis shows that matters stood quite differently.

We registered, by continuous recording,* all the words the twins used during eight uninterrupted sessions in order to find out the frequency with which they used words natural to common speech and words which did not have a permanent, stable meaning. It appeared that these groups of words were not both used with the same frequency. As is shown in Table 2, out of 194 expressions used by one, and 202 by the other twin brother we were able to record only 72 (and correspondingly 65) separate, often repeated words. However, if we isolate the words which recur most often it appears that 8–10 words occupied a predominant place in the twins' speech and that these are not clear objective words but all words which do not possess a constant meaning and are comprehensible only in a particular situation.

Table 2 Frequency of Repetition of
Separate Words by Twins G

	Twin A	Twin B
Total number of words pronounced	194	202
Number of different words recorded	72	65
Repetition of separate words:		
Liosia	24	21
Liulia	21	21
Net (No)	11	6
Ne (Not)	14	9
Tut (Here)	9	9
Tak (So)	5	10
Seichas (Now)	4	
Vot, Von (Here is, there is)		8
Davai (Give me)		7
Nado (I want)		7

*That is, by taking a verbatim record during the observation.

Here, besides the names of the twins, 'Liosia' and 'Liulia', are such common words as 'not', 'no', 'here', 'so' etc. But they acquired an entirely different meaning when they were pronounced in different situations and in a different tone of voice. Thus the word 'Liosia' could mean: 'I (Liosha) am playing nicely', or 'Let him (Liosha) go for a walk', or 'Look (Liosha) what I have done'.

As is shown in Table 3 this use of names, possessing an entirely different meaning in different circumstances, constituted from 20 to 23 per cent of the twins' speech; other words which did not in themselves possess a distinct meaning and acquired meaning only from the situation (e.g. 'tak', 'ntsa', 'aga', 'eh' etc.) constituted nearly half the twins' speech.

Words of common speech denoting objects (frequently having, as we have noted, a diffuse meaning) did not exceed 27 to 33 per cent of the total words recorded. Thus it can be seen that three-quarters of the language of our twins consisted of their own names and expressive-indicatory exclamations, having a diffuse, impermanent meaning; while words of common speech, denoting things, in practice constituted only a small proportion of their expressions.

These data illustrate the basic characteristic of the children's speech; *as a rule our twins' speech acquired meaning only in a concrete-active situation.* Outside this situation a word either did not possess any kind of permanent meaning, or only indicated

Table 3 Semantics of the Words of Twins G during the First Period of Observation

Group of words	Twin A		Twin B	
	Number of words	Frequency of repetition	Number of words	Frequency of repetition
Names of the twins	2 (2·8%)	45 (23·3%)	2 (3·2%)	41 (20·8%)
Words with diffuse meaning	30 (41·6%)	92 (47·4%)	27 (41·4%)	91 (44·5%)
Naming of objects	38 (52·8%)	53 (27·2%)	34 (52·2%)	67 (33·2%)
Corresponding (grammatical) word	2 (2·8%)	4 (2·1%)	2 (3·2%)	3 (1·5%)
Total	72	194	65	202

what they were talking about without disclosing sufficiently clearly in what sense it was being used.

Thus the unit of their speech was not yet an independently distinguished word, but a word which acquired meaning only in an active situation. One and the same word might possess an entirely different meaning in different situations and outside a particular situation this meaning could not be understood.

Several passages of the children's speech may serve to illustrate this.

1. Liosha (showing the teacher a pattern he has made with a mosaic): 'Liosia, vo, ntsa, aga, ntsa' (meaning: 'Look how well I've done it. Isn't it good?')

Liosha (looking at a picture which represents an adult giving something to a child, addressing Yura): 'Aga, papa, Liosia, ntsa, aga?' (i.e. 'Papa is giving Liosha something nice, yes?')

2. Yura, approaching some playing children; 'Liulia, Liulia' (i.e. 'I (Yura) will play too')

Yura, giving Liosha a sheet of paper: 'Liulia, Liulia' (i.e. 'draw me something')

These examples show that one and the same expression acquired a different meaning in different situations and that to evaluate this meaning outside the situation was impossible.

In a number of cases the children's speech consisted wholly in expressive exclamations or names. And in these cases the meaning of the expressions became comprehensible only in the light of the situation.

Twin A (Yura)

1. Not satisfied with something Liosha has done in play, he gesticulates and says, raising his voice: 'Ne nàta, ne nàta, ne nàta tak' (i.e. 'Don't do that').

2. Another boy is sitting on a car with which he is playing and Yura pushes him, reddens, and cries on one note: 'Ee-ee-ee.'

3. Playing, and shifting a toy from place to place: 'Vo-vo-vo-nazad' (i.e. 'Here ... back').

4. After this, when a paper toy is given to him: 'Liulia posaia, posaia' (for bolshaia, bigger).

5. Considering a toy which has been made: 'Liulia, liutze, Liulia, liutze' (for luchshe, better).

Twin B (Liosha)

1. Calling Yura into a room where he is supposed to play: 'Liulia, Liulia, Liosia, tut' ('Yura, Yura, Liosha, here').
2. Explaining to the teacher that Yura does not want to come: 'Net, Liulia, net' ('No, Yura, no').
3. Crawling into a box and inviting Yura from there: 'Stsiac (for seichas, now), Liulia, Liosia, Liulia, oi.'
4. In play divides the table into two halves: 'Ne Liosia mesmia' (for mesto, i.e. 'No, this is Liosha's place').
5. Not wanting to stay any longer in the same room as the teacher: 'Liosha ne nata tut' (i.e. 'I do not want to stay here any longer').

An analysis of the role of such amorphous expressions in the children's speech is given in Table 4. This table shows that amorphous-expressive sentences, incomprehensible outside the immediate situation, constituted the major proportion (82·6 and 78·2 per cent) of the words used by the twins and that differentiated, comprehensible sentences appeared comparatively rarely.

Table 4 Character of the Expressions of Twins G and Degree of Objectivity of Speech

Construction of sentences	Twin A	Twin B
Amorphous-expressive sentences incomprehensible outside a situation	57 (82·6%)	54 (78·2%)
1. diffuse (without objective words)	31 (45%)	24 (34·7%)
2. short, ungrammatical sentences (with objective words)	26 (37·6%)	30 (43·5%)
Differentiated (objective) sentences (comprehensible outside a situation)	12 (17·4%)	15 (21·8%)
1. ungrammatical	6 (8·7%)	8 (11·6%)
2. grammatical	6 (8·7%)	7 (10·2%)

The grammar of the children's 'autonomous' speech

Analysis of the children's expressions leads on directly to the question of the grammatical structure of their speech.

The fact that the speech of both twins was still not developed as an independent activity of communication with the aid of language, but always constituted a fragment of a concrete-active situation outside which it was incomprehensible, determined its grammatical structure.

It is essential to recognize that such 'synpraxic' speech cannot have an independent grammar, that the 'grammar' of the child's autonomous speech is, indeed, the child's concrete activity as a whole. The word is interlocked with this activity and sometimes plays the role of object (while the subject remains in the concrete-active situation), or indicates an object which is being spoken about when it is the subject that is replaced by concrete gestures and by the child's actions. In this connection it will be understood that a significant majority of our children's expressions consisted either of primitive sentences of an amorphous type, or sentences in which, despite the presence of meaningful words, one of the most important parts of speech – the subject or object – was absent, being subsumed and only disclosed in the active situation. The corresponding data are set out in Table 5.

We can see from this that amorphous sentences constituted the major proportion of expressions and that grammatically developed sentences constituted only an insignificant proportion of the twins' speech.

No special explanation is needed of the fact that the amorphous phrase in the child's autonomous speech is characterized by a complete absence of grammatical features in the connection of words, and that words joined with a common action-meaning are not as a rule marshalled in a clear grammatical sequence requiring inflections, conjunctions etc. Even in cases when the child manages to express a complex correlation of facts, his autonomous speech does not go beyond the limit of ungrammatical 'attachments'.

An example is a situation when, attempting to find a toy dog, Liosha separately pronounces the words: 'Este (eshche), sapàtka (sobachka), este netou sapàtka' ('Still not dog'; i.e. 'the dog isn't here').

Thus the twins' speech during this first phase of observation was synpraxic in its meaning and ungrammatical in structure.

Table 5 Grammatical Structure of Sentences of Twins G (Frequency of Grammatically Developed Speech)

Types of sentence	Twin A	Twin B
Amorphous sentences	43 (62·3%)	37 (53·6%)
1. single word[a]	18 (26·1%)	20 (29%)
2. extended amorphous[b]	25 (36·2%)	17 (24·6%)
Semi-differentiated sentences	14 (20·3%)	20 (29·0%)
1. sentences without a predicate[c]	12 (17·4%)	16 (23·2%)
2. sentences without a subject[d]	2 (2·9%)	4 (5·8%)
Grammatically complete sentences	12 (17·4%)	12 (17·4%)
1. complete but not extended	4 (5·8%)	4 (5·8%)
2. complete, extended sentences (with object, attribute etc.)	8 (11·6%)	8 (11·6%)
Total number of sentences	69	69

(a) e.g. 'Mitka' for mishka (bear).
(b) e.g. 'Liulia, Liosia, aga, ntsa'.
(c) e.g. 'Liulia ... liasatka' ('Yura ... horse').
(d) e.g. 'Ne nata ...' ('Don't do ...').

The function of 'autonomous' speech

The data given above show clearly that the functions of our twins' speech, which was interlocked with action, differed sharply from the functions characteristic of adult speech, or even that of pre-school children.

Soviet psychologists, taking their departure from Pavlov's finding concerning the interaction of the two signal systems, have shown the variety of functions speech fulfils when participating directly in the formation of mental processes.

Their investigations have not only shown that the word participates in the process of active reflection of reality, ensuring the most complex forms of abstraction and generalization of real stimūli; more recently they have also upheld the view that the most complex forms of the child's orienting activity are formed with the participation of speech. The child's speech begins to participate by regulating motions and actions, then secures the transition to complex forms of meaningful play and ends by becoming the most important factor in the development of conscious behaviour. Research has shown that the development in children of the orienting, and with this the regulating, functions of speech can be traced with considerable exactitude at four to four and a half years of age; just at this age it is possible to observe the intimate participation of speech in establishing new connections, in verbal control of inhibitory processes etc.[22]

Obviously, because of the peculiarities of their speech processes, our twins were deficient in so far as they lacked the function of full-value speech in the reflection of reality and in the regulation of their activity.

All the functions of speech mentioned above remained limited in so far as in their case the word was insufficiently detached from action, diffuse in its meaning, and there was not yet developed, full-value speech.

In the case of our twins, then, the word could not reflect the external situation with the objectivity, generalization and profundity characteristic of speech at a higher stage of development. Their undeveloped speech could not carry out the independent function of complex orientation which is reflected in full-value narration. Finally, their speech was interconnected with direct action, had not yet developed into an independent system and so, naturally, could not fulfil the role of regulation, of planning future behaviour, which is characteristic of the speech of the normal child of the same age.

In Table 6 a summary is given of the twins' speech. It will be seen that in 92 to 94 per cent of instances it is synpraxic speech,

fragmented expressive requests, wishes and evaluations, ful-
filling the function of indicating objects which participate in an
operative situation. Planning and narrative speech were almost
completely absent in our twins.

The following examples of the twins' expressions show clearly
that narrative and planning functions were quite alien to their
primitive, undeveloped speech. The first two examples belong to
affective speech – requests; the two latter represent the indicatory,
denotary function of speech.

1. The children are making paper doves. Yura turns to a child Valusha;
'Liulia, Liulia, Valusia, Liulia' (i.e. 'Valusha, make one for me too').

2. In play in an analogous situation, Yura turns to another child
Vasia: 'Net, on.' ('No, him', i.e. 'No, let him do it').

3. Liosha, doing something with a toy horse: 'Vo, liasiatka' (for 'Vot
loshadka'; 'Here is the horse').

4. Talking about the teacher who is writing something, pointing to
her; 'Liosia, aga-a, Liosia, Liulia, tak.'

Table 6 Functional Analysis of the Speech of Twins G

Forms of speech	Twin A	Twin B
	%	%
1. Synpraxic speech (connected with action)	92·9	94·3
(a) requests, wishes, evaluatory, commentary, etc.	39·3	42·2
(b) indicatory, affirmatory	53·6	52·1
2. Planning speech (regulating the child's behaviour)	4·3	4·3
(a) within the bounds of a situation	4·3	4·3
(b) anticipatory	0	0
3. Narrative speech	2·8	1·4
(a) connected with a situation (descriptive)	0	0
(b) not connected with a situation (recollective, imaginative)	2·8	1·4
Speech connected with a situation (1a, 1b; 2a; 3a)	97·2	98·6
Speech transcending the bounds of a situation (2b; 3b)	2·8	1·4

The beginnings of planning speech, regulating future activity, are very seldom to be discerned; usually they find a place in the active situation and do not reach beyond such expressions as: 'Liosia tavai tak' ('Liosha, give it'), 'Liulia bliasat, a ty tut' ('Yura throw here, you here').

It will be noted that nearly all the twins' speech remains connected with the child's direct action in a particular situation. It either expresses the child's relation to this situation or indicates, denotes, the things directly participating in this concrete situation. We do not yet find either narrative speech or speech which transcends the boundaries of a situation and plans future action. All this indicates that our twins' speech cannot in any sense be called really developed, objective speech, that it is not in itself an independent activity singled out from the child's direct behaviour.

Comprehension of extraneous speech

It is now necessary to throw some light on another important question: how was an understanding of extraneous speech formed in our twins when their own speech was so primitive? If the twins' active speech was nearly always interlocked in a situation, did this mean that extraneous speech was only comprehensible to them in cases when it was directly addressed to them and so was also interlocked with a concrete, practical situation?

Our first observations concerning the twins' understanding of extraneous speech led us to the opposite conclusion. At first it seemed that the children's understanding of this was secure and did not differ from their understanding of each other's speech. However, careful investigation showed that, while our twins understood perfectly speech that was directly related to an object or action which preoccupied them, they were not in a position to understand speech when it was not directly connected with a concrete situation and took a developed, narrative form. Thus their understanding of extraneous speech was subject to the same regularities as was the construction of their own speech.

In order to find out precisely how adequately the children understood the meanings of separate words, we carried out several special investigations. If the instructor suggested that they pick out some named object or picture they did this easily and it seemed that the recollective aspect of the perceived word had full value for them. However, it was only necessary to name an object which was absent for our twins to show a marked difference from their counterparts of the same age. The latter were now confused and refused to point to anything, but our twins often pointed at one of the objects before them and in so doing revealed the instability and diffuseness of meaning of words in their case. For instance, they would point correctly to a tram, an axe, a dog, a stove; but when asked, where is the calf? where is the lamb? – these objects being absent in the actual situation – they would point again at the dog, or if asked to denote a chair would point at a table, so indicating the *generalized character of verbal meanings*.

Understanding of elementary grammatical relations within the bounds of the visual situation was secure. The children could even understand questions which did not name the object they had to point out. Thus, they correctly pointed to the corresponding object when asked the following questions: 'What does the axe chop?' (Firewood); 'What do you write with?' (A pencil); 'Whose spectacles are these?' (Uncle's) etc. They easily understood a question requiring description of an object and produced adequately descriptive gestures in answer to such questions as: 'What shape is this coin?', 'What shape is this ruler?' etc. They appeared to be sufficiently sensitive to the inflections of verbs which they did not use in their own speech. For example, one of the twins asked a question: 'Mama visiped koupil?' ('Has mother bought a bicycle?').* The instructor, in reply, queried 'Koupila?' and he protested 'Net, koupil', but when the instructor again queried 'Koupit?' he cheerfully answered 'Da' ('Yes').

However, the impression gained from initial answers as to the complete security of the twins' understanding of speech was wrong. It was only necessary to depass the bounds of the elementary, indicatory function in sentences addressed to them, to make a transition to speech unconnected with the direct

*The child was trying to ask 'Mama velosiped koupit?' ('Will Mama buy a bicycle?'). But instead of the future tense 'koupit' he incorrectly used the masculine of the past tense 'koupil', the feminine being 'koupila'. [Ed.]

situation, for it to become clear that these complex forms of speech were no longer understood by our children.

This defective understanding was revealed as soon as we turned to the developed sentence, which could only be understood if there were comparison of its separate words and inhibition of a reaction to some single word snatched from its context. In these cases, comprehension of the developed sentence as a complex verbal stimulus was often replaced by a direct reaction to some separate link, and the child answered with a single word which had figured in the question, ignoring its complex grammatical structure. Thus, during play, performing a scene which represented a trip in a boat up the river to a forest, one of the twins was asked: 'Where are Mama and Liosha going?' He answered: 'the boat', obviously replacing the necessary answer by a simple indication of the object 'in which they were going'. An analogous answer was given by the other twin who was asked during play which represented a journey by tram to the hospital: 'Where are Mama and Yura going?' and answered 'in the tram'.

Deficiencies in understanding were more clearly revealed in cases when our twins heard a phrase in which only one element was singled out from the immediate situation while the accomplishment of the instructions given involved several actions not indicated in the sentence. One example may serve as an illustration. The child, who was occupied in choosing subject pictures from a heap lying before him, was told: 'Put the ball here'. If this task was so constructed that the child had to find the picture of the ball among the heap of pictures before him, he was silent, obviously not understanding the task and remaining confused. However, if the child was given direct instructions whereby the task was divided into two separate parts – 'Find the ball' and 'Put it here' – he accomplished first one, then the other, immediately and successfully. Even when the child was given a double but direct instruction of the type – 'Take out this picture and put the ball here' – he easily fulfilled these tasks. Thus *speech was completely comprehensible if it did not go beyond the bounds of the visual situation* and *did not become a complex stimulus which sometimes necessitated an intermediate action.* But it became incomprehensible if some fragment of the instructions was abstracted from the immediate situation and action and transcended the bounds of direct reaction.

By reason of this, understanding of developed, narrative speech often remained inaccessible to our children. In these cases they often snatched at an element of the sentence, failing to relate this to the general context, which obviously led to misunderstanding of the content of the instructions.

A single example will be sufficient to indicate the frontiers delimiting their understanding of speech. When the child who led their group came up and said 'Liosha and Yura, put on your shoes we are going to dance', they began to cry, which astonished the leader because she knew they loved dancing. But when the twins were given a direct, concrete explanation: 'Auntie Maia and Auntie Olia have come, so now we're going to dance', Yura stopped crying and began to explain 'Liosia, en, Maia, Olia, Maia, en ...' and the twins quickly began to get ready. The narrative phrase, being a complex verbal stimulus, was incomprehensible to the twins and called forth a reaction not to its own meaning but to the situation (put on your shoes and go somewhere); only mention of the teachers' names and Yura's primitive 'translation' provided an opportunity for understanding it.

Such deficient understanding of developed speech meant that the children in fact never heard a conversation or the teacher's reading. When the other children gathered round the teacher to listen to a story the twins G began to play with each other and attempts to draw them to listen to narrative speech met with no success.

Thus the impression that they had a complete understanding of speech addressed to them was obviously incorrect and these observations convinced us that their understanding of speech was limited to snatching at the direct meaning of separate words and to attempts to single out from the situation the significance of instructions addressed to them. As in the case of their independent speech, so also their perception of extraneous speech was connected with the direct, actual situation and was delimited to direct reactions to the meaning of separate words.

Chapter 5
Experimental Development of the Speech of Twins G and Its Effect

It has already been suggested that two factors lay at the basis of the retarded speech development of the twins under observation; firstly, a predisposition to retardation of speech connected with phonetical impairment, and secondly, the 'twin situation' which did not create an objective necessity for the development of speech as a special means of communication.

If this proposition were correct then it could be supposed that it would be sufficient to separate the twins for a certain time – placing them in different groups in the kindergarten and thus removing that type of direct communication which hindered their speech development – in order to create an objective necessity for the development of speech; that, in such circumstances, retarded speech would develop to a stage corresponding to that of a normal child of the same age.

In order to establish the specific weight of the former factor – the speech defect (which we shall consider in more detail)* – we introduced supplementary conditions into our experiment. Having separated the children, and thus created a situation which impelled them into speech communication, we singled out one of the twins – Yura (the weaker one, as has already been indicated) – and began to give him special speech training with the aim of developing a better differentiation of sounds, better pronunciation and, of paramount importance, the acquisition of a developed speech system.

*The speech defect of the twins G was characterized by complex phonetic impairment manifested in a disturbance of the differentiation of closely related consonants, difficulties in pronouncing affricates, the running together of consonants and so on.

The method used in the experimental development of speech

The lessons were as follows. The child was first encouraged to give answers to questions, then required actively to name objects, and finally actively to answer questions, to repeat complete phrases and to describe pictures. The instruction continued for three months, then there was a break of two months; afterwards instruction was renewed and continued for a further six months.

A few passages from our records will show the exercises given at the beginning of the course and some of those given a few months later. The first extract belongs to the beginning of the course.

Instructor	*Yura*
'Good morning Yura.'	Silently stretches his hand.
'Well, good morning Yura.'	Silent.
'Did you come by tram?'	Silent.
'Did Yura come in the tramcar?'	Silent.
'Who did Yura come with?'	Silent.
'With Uncle Vania?'	Shakes head negatively.
'Who did Yura come with? With Fania Yakovlevna?'	Nods head silently.
'Yes, Yura came with Auntie Fania!'	Same reaction.
'What is Yura wearing today? Boots' (pointing).	Yura silently looks on.
'Yes, boots and socks.'	Yura silently looks on and smiles.

In short, the usual answers to questions addressed to him were practical actions always accompanied by silence.

After three months' instruction the same exercises produced essentially different results.

Instructor	*Yura*
'Yura, please give me the car.'	Silently hands the toy.
'No, I shall not take it like that. Say, "Auntie Luda, take the car"' (avto).	'Auntie, take the car' (ato).

'Yes, the car (avto). Now Yura?'   'Car' (afto).
'Now you ask!'   'Give me the elephant' (silon).
'No, not like that. Say:
"Auntie Luda, please give me the
elephant"' (slon).   'Auntie Luda, give . . . the
elephant' (silon).

'Good. Here is the elephant.'
'Yura, please give me the
aeroplane' (samolet, which the
instructor pronounces by
syllables, sa-mo-let).   'Take the aeroplane'
(sa-mo-let).

Finally, after ten months of instruction the child's speech communication took an entirely different form.

Instructor	*Yura*
Picture 1	
'Who is that, a boy?'	'No.'
'Who then?'	'A grandfather' (tetuska, for diedushka).
'What is he doing?'	'He is reading a book' (k'nizku, for knigu).
'A book?'	'A newspaper' (kazetu, for gazetu).
Picture 2	
'What is this?'	'A squirrel' (pelotska, for belochka).
'How do you know it is a squirrel?'	'The tail is so bushy' (pusistyi, for pushistyi).
'Where does she live?'	'The forest.'
'In the forest?'	'In the forest.'
'But where does she live in the forest?'	Silent.
'Does she have a house?'	'She does.'
'Where?'	'On the tree' (delevo, for diereve).
'How on the tree?'	'In a hole' (dylke, for duple).
'In a hole?'	Silent.

The construction of the experiment just described enabled us to make a double check; to verify the improvements which appeared in the speech of both children and to compare these improvements with the peculiarities of their speech before they were separated.

If there were an equivalent improvement in both twins this would enable us to evaluate the role played by the 'twin situation' in retarding speech development and the variations called forth in the twins' speech by the appearance of a new and great impetus to speech development. Comparing the development in the speech of each twin after three months' separation and after one of them had begun a course of speech training, we could assess the role played by the supplementary teaching of one of the twins and the extent to which his development had been influenced by the formation of habits of speech communication.

We checked the development of the twins' speech after three months and again ten months after the beginning of the experiment. We shall hereafter designate the twin who was given speech training (Yura) as Twin A and the 'control' twin (Liosha) as Twin B.

Variations in the function of speech in twins G after their separation

Observations carried out during the first months of our experiment showed that the very separation of the twins created an objective necessity for the development of their speech; nonverbal forms of communication, which were formerly predominant, were now obviously insufficient for communication with other people. In order to be understood, each twin, included in the general life of the kindergarten, must inevitably come to speak in order to express his wishes, to participate in play and to avoid being completely excluded from the new form of the collective.

The results of their changed conditions of life were soon apparent. At first our twins were silent, then they gradually began to take part in the common life of the child collective and to speak. In the third month of the experiment, speech interlocked with the practical situation and speech which was incomprehensible outside a situation retreated into the background, giving place to various forms of speech in which the elements of 'autonomous' speech had already ceased to play an important part and the predominant place was taken by forms of speech communication proper to this age. It is interesting to note that these improvements appeared in the control Twin B as well as in the trained Twin A, which enabled us to evaluate them as the resultant of the new situation which objectively impelled the children into speech communication.

Here is an example of the twins' speech after three months of the experiment. All these sentences are still inadequate, both in pronunciation and grammatically,* but now they take the form of extended phrases, with subject, predicate and object.

Twin A
1. During play; ('Ia kotel tomik ne vislo') 'I wanted a house, didn't get it.'
2. Constructing a building, looking at a cube; ('Ia takoi potiavit') 'I put on this one.'
3. In play; ('Holoso liapan') 'A good aeroplane.'

Twin B
1. Modelling; ('Liosia deliait tsolik') 'Liosha's making a table.'
2. Same; ('Ia umeit makoku') 'I can do a carrot.'
3. Drawing; ('Liulia, ne nata potet') 'Yura mustn't look.'

It can be seen that the twins' speech has not only become notably more comprehensible but that they are beginning to use, in significantly greater degree, the common words of the language. Special interest attaches to the fact that not only the vocabulary of their speech but also its function now became radically different. Before the experiment began most of our twins' speech was not differentiated from direct action and only accompanied this action; now new functions appeared, orienting, planning and also narrative speech began to play a significant part in their communication.

Table 7 summarizes the results of observations undertaken

*The translation does not convey either mispronunciation or incorrect use of verbs. [Ed.]

after three months and after ten months of the experiment. From this it can be seen that before the experiment began synpraxic speech, interlocked with direct action, constituted from 92 to 94 per cent of the twins' expressions but that after three months' separation its specific weight was sharply reduced. In Twin A it constituted only 44·2 per cent, in Twin B 60·7 per cent, of all expressions. Thus, while there were originally only insignificant differences between the twins in the place occupied by synpraxic speech, certain differences appeared in the course of the experiment. Control Twin B retained more 'synpraxic' expressions than the trained Twin A, but nevertheless there was also a significant reduction in the specific weight of primitive speech, interlocked with practical action, in both twins.

Further analysis of the table shows which forms of speech

Table 7 Comparative Analysis of the Functions of Speech Before and After Separation of Twins G

Forms of speech	Before separation		After 3 months' separation		After 10 months' separation	
	A	B	A	B	A	B
Number of sentences recorded	69	69	102	32	45	58
	%	%	%	%	%	%
1. Synpraxic speech (connected with direct action)	92·8	94·1	44·2	60·7	33·2	25·8
(a) requests, wishes, evaluation	39·2	42·0	11·2	12·1	6·4	10·3
(b) indicatory, descriptive	53·6	52·1	27·4	33·5	26·8	15·5
(c) questions, in play	0	0	5·6	15·1	0	0
2. Planning speech	4·4	4·3	40·0	36·3	45·9	46·5
(a) within the bounds of a situation	4·4	4·3	16·6	21·2	10·5	24·1
(b) anticipatory	0	0	23·4	15·1	35·4	22·4
3. Narrative speech	2·8	1·6	15·8	3	20·9	27·7
(a) connected with a situation	0	0	15·8	3	4·3	22·4
(b) not connected with a situation	2·8	1·6	0	0	16·6	5·3
Speech transcending the bounds of a situation (2b; 3b)	2·8	1·6	23·4	15·1	52·0	27·7

improved equally in both twins, and which improvements can be assigned to the special factor of training Twin A. We may notice that in both children orienting, planning speech, which not only accompanied but also anticipated the corresponding activity, improved in an equal degree.

At the outset of the experiment such speech was virtually absent (it did not exceed 4 per cent of all the twins' expressions); but now more than a third of all their speech (40 per cent in one and 36 per cent in the other) began to be related to this category. It is clear, therefore, that removal of the twin situation led to a rapid development of planning speech in both twins.

However, it is characteristic that the role of planning speech only increased to an insignificant degree in the following months, and ten months after the beginning of the experiment only constituted 45 to 46 per cent of all expressions.

The peculiarity of this further development is that in the following months complex, anticipatory speech began to take a more significant place by comparison with forms of planning speech which remained within the bounds of an operative situation. Three months after the outset of the experiment the latter predominated, but after ten months it began to give place to more complex functional speech, with an orienting role which transcended the bounds of an immediate situation.

In the case of that other form of speech, which we have called narrative, matters stood differently. This kind of speech, almost completely absent earlier, constituted 15·8 per cent in the case of Twin A after three months but had hardly developed at all in Twin B. This convincingly suggests that the appearance of planning speech was the direct result of the new objective situation, in which speech lost its connection with direct action, but that the development of narrative speech at this first stage was the direct result of speech training.

Ten months after the beginning of the experiment narrative speech appeared in both twins, but now Twin A, who had been trained, began to acquire complex forms of narrative speech not connected with the immediate situation, while in control Twin B narrative speech remained more closely connected with the immediate situation and was not usually detached from it.

All this shows that speech disconnected from action could enter into new relations with the child's activity and thus acquire new functions.

Another important finding is directly relevant here. Very soon after the experiment began, amorphous expressions, incomprehensible outside the immediate situation, rapidly retreated into the background, giving place to objective speech which was comprehensible outside the situation.

This is shown in Table 8.

At first, expressions which were comprehensible outside an immediate situation hardly exceeded 17 to 21 per cent, but after three months they constituted 81 to 88 per cent of all expressions while only 12 to 19 per cent of expressions remained amorphous.

This indicates that removal of the twin situation called forth an essential change in the structure, as well as the function, of speech; the twins' speech was transformed into speech proper to their age which utilized the generally accepted speech system; and, it is particularly important to note, this change took place within a very short period.

Changes in the structure of the twins' speech

The foregoing findings indicate that the removal of the twin situation inevitably called forth essential improvements, not only

Table 8 Degree of Comprehensibility Outside an Active Context of Sentences of Twins G

Sentences	Before separation		After 3 months' separation		After 10 months' separation	
	A	B	A	B	A	B
Total number of sentences	69	69	102	32	45	58
Incomprehensible outside a situation (amorphous)	%	%	%	%	%	%
	82·6	78·2	11·4	18·8	0	0
Comprehensible outside a situation (notional)	17·4	21·8	88·6	81·2	100	100

in the function but also in the grammatical structure of speech; diffused, amorphous speech began to be replaced by a normal, grammatical language system.

Table 9 gives a summary of the corresponding observations.

As has been noted, originally the major proportion of the twins' expressions consisted in amorphous phrases, in which for the most part objective words found no place. But after three months of the experiment these phrases rapidly fell into the background. Now only 12 to 19 per cent of all expressions still bore an amorphous character and only in 3 per cent of cases did the twins' speech continue to have the character of expressions interlocked with practical activity which lacked any objective words. At the outset of the experiment more than one-third of all the twins' expressions were related to this group. By contrast, differentiated phrases, which originally constituted not more than 17 to 21 per cent of all their speech, now began to constitute 81 to 88 per cent of the whole. Thus, removal of the twin situation and the new objective necessity for speech communication called forth differentiated sentences in both children.

The influence of speech training was noticed only in the character of differentiated expressions; in control Twin B only 36 per cent of all differentiated sentences began to bear a gram-

Table 9 Changes in the Grammatical structure of the Speech of Twins G Before and After Separation

Structural forms of speech	Before separation		After 3 months' separation		After 10 months' separation	
	A	B	A	B	A	B
Total number of sentences	69	69	102	32	45	58
	%	%	%	%	%	%
Amorphous sentences	82·6	78·2	11·4	18·8	0	0
1. diffuse (without objective words)	45·0	34·7	3·0	3·0	0	0
2. (with objective words)	37·6	43·5	8·4	15·8	0	0
Differentiated sentences	17·4	21·8	88·6	81·2	100	100
1. ungrammatical	8·7	11·6	26·1	45·1	15·5	17·0
2. grammatical	8·7	10·2	62·5	36·1	84·5	83·0

matical character while in 45 per cent of cases the sentence remained ungrammatical, but in Twin A the ungrammatical sentence began to be met with in only 26 per cent of cases while the grammatically constructed phrase began to occupy a predominant place and was met in 62 per cent of cases.

Ten months after the beginning of the experiment these differences were levelled out, giving place to other, sectional differences. These more specific differences which appeared as one result of training are summarized in Table 10.

Table 10 Quantity of Developed Grammatical Sentences in the Speech of Twins G Before and After Separation (Percentage)

Degree of development of sentence	Before separation		After 3 months' separation		After 10 months' separation	
	A	B	A	B	A	B
Unextended sentences	25·8	34·8	33·9	59·4	9	52
Extended sentences	11·6	11·6	54·7	21·8	91	48

Here we can see that the twins' speech before the experiment consisted mainly in unextended sentences, that after three months simple sentences continued to form the greater part of control of Twin B's speech, while in Twin A they gave place to extended sentences; these differences between the twins remained clearly noticeable even after ten months of the experiment.

If, then, the new objective necessity for speech communication led to the appearance of objective speech, special training called forth differentiated, developed sentences.

We may give here comparative examples of different forms of the twins' speech after three months and after ten months of the experiment. These will assist an evaluation of the summary data set out above.*

*In these examples, incorrect pronunciation, which is very characteristic of the children's Russian speech, must be assumed; but an attempt has been made to indicate incorrect grammatical construction. [Ed.]

Observations After Three Months' Separation of the Twins

1. Developed grammatical speech

Twin A

(a) Playing with a mosaic; 'Look I have a boat . . . I'm making another boat.'

(b) Same situation; 'I'm making a wheel now.'

Twin B

(a) 'How the engine sounds fast . . .'

(b) 'We have none . . .' (cubes).

2. Undeveloped grammatical speech

Twin A

(a) ('Stias ia liodku') 'Now I a boat' i.e. 'Now I'll make a boat.'

(b) ('Titskin tomik') 'Bird's house' i.e. 'I've made a bird's house.'

Twin B

(a) Proposing to his companion that he carry some cubes; ('Ehali') 'We go.'

(b) Modelling; ('Liosia kopatku') 'Liosha a sausage' i.e. 'I shall make a sausage.'

(c) Same situation; ('Schas flag') 'Now a flag.'

3. Ungrammatical speech

Twin A

(a) ('Liosha net doma delit') 'Liosha no make house' i.e. 'Liosha isn't making a house.'

(b) ('Aga, ia tavit') 'Aga me stand' i.e. 'I'm standing up.'

(c) ('Schas ia delil temno-temno') 'Now I made dark-dark' i.e. 'Now I'm making it dark.'

Twin B

(a) ('Schas Liulia mashina, Liosia sofel') 'Now Liulia engine, Liosia driver' i.e. 'Now Yura is the engine, Liosha is the driver.'

(b) ('Kolo okliasit kubiki') 'Soon he paints the cubes' i.e. 'They will soon paint the cubes.'

Observations After Ten Months' Separation of the Twins

Twin A

'We have a picture, a boy flies on a parachute . . .'

'It's a picture . . . a boy lost himself in a wood . . . he shouted "ow", he called the children. It's interesting. We went on the merry-go-round with papa. I said to papa: "Let's go on the merry-go-round" then we bought tickets and went in the metro.'

Twin B
'The fish drunk water ... a worm jumped up ... he swallowed it ...'
'You remember we went ... the barge, a long way ...'
'The engine one headlight ...' (i.e. 'There is one headlight on the engine').

Development in the comprehension of extraneous speech

The removal of the 'twin situation' led to remarkable progress not only in the structure of the twins' expressive speech but also in the development of their comprehension of extraneous speech.

Initially the twins' comprehension of extraneous speech was sharply delimited; speech detached from direct practical action, which was not directly addressed to them or was grammatically complex in some way, was often not perceived by them. But once they were included in a situation of speech communication the twins came not only to use speech for active communication but also the boundaries of their understanding of speech addressed to them were significantly widened.

Now, as our observations showed, they more willingly and actively took part in extraneous conversation, willingly listened to reading aloud and began to perceive, like the other children, the meaning of tasks set by the teacher. After only three to four months of the experiment we could not easily single out our twins from the other children and were hardly able to point to an example of lack of comprehension of extraneous speech.

In this respect there was no particular difference between Twin A and control Twin B. Differences arose only in the course of special experiments which showed that Twin A, under the influence of speech training, had developed the capacity to make specific speech structures an object of perception and to master the meaning of complex grammatical structures a great deal more freely than Twin B.

We undertook several additional control experiments with both children. First they were given instructions which did not include inflectional relations; e.g. 'pokazhi grebeshok, karandash' ('show the comb, the pencil' etc.). Then inflectional relations were included; 'pokazhi grebeshkom karandash' (literally, 'show *with* the comb – the pencil'). Sometimes the latter instruction was given in an easier form in that, to facilitate understanding of the relations of inflections, the pointing particle was added; 'pokazhi grebeshkom *na* karandash' ('Point with the comb *at* the pencil'). Then both twins were given sentences composed of the same words but not placed in the same order. These varied in structure being either active or passive; e.g. 'Petia oudaril Vasi*u*' ('Petia hit Vasia') or 'Peti*u* oudaril Vasia' ('Petia was hit by Vasia') with the subsequent question 'Who was the bully?' Consequently these sentences were not equally difficult.[23]

Our observations showed that there were notable differences between the twins in perception and analysis of sentences involving complex grammatical relations. Control Twin B was often unable to differentiate grammatical constructions, but Twin A was in a position to make the grammatical constructions an object of perception and to differentiate sufficiently exactly the relations they expressed.

Comparative examples, which show the differences called forth by speech training of both twins, are given below.

Understanding of the relations of inflections

Twin A

1. Constructions with no inflection are carried out without difficulty.

2. With the transition to instructions involving inflections he easily passes from successive pointing at objects to pointing with an object to an object; nevertheless he often confuses the relation of objects; e.g. 'pokazhi karandash grebeshk*om*' ('show the pencil *with* the comb') – points with the pencil to the comb.

3. Instructions with a particle; e.g. 'pokazhi karandashom *na* grebeshok' ('point with the pencil *at* the comb') he differentiates at once and perfectly understands the meaning of the sentence.

Twin B

1. Constructions with no inflection are carried out without difficulty.

2. With the transition to instructions involving inflections he shows no improvement. Continues to point to both objects mentioned: e.g.

'pokazhi kliuch*om* karandash' ('show *with* the key – the pencil') – points to both key and pencil.

3. Even the introduction of the easier particle 'at' does not produce any improvement; however, after special training he begins easily to carry out instructions.

4. After this training, a return to instructions 1 and 2 does not produce differentiation and the child in both cases understands the instruction as inflected; even inclusion of the conjunction 'and', e.g. 'pokazhi karandash i kliuch' ('show the pencil and the key') does not produce a transition to successive pointing with the objects; it is obvious that the transposition of words – 'kliuchom karandash', 'karandashom kliuch' ('with the key – the pencil', 'with the pencil – the key') – is not differentiated; in both cases the child perceives the first of the objects mentioned as active and the second as the object to be shown.

Understanding of the grammatical meaning of the order of words in a sentence

Twin A

1. A sentence with a simple grammatical construction is easily understood. But a sentence with an inverted (passive) construction is not correctly understood. e.g. 'Peti*u* pobil Vasia. Kto drachoun?' ('Petia was struck by Vasia. Who was the bully?') – 'Petia'.

2. The repetition of sentences with an inverted structure shows that the subject perceives the transposition of words and attempts to reproduce it (though unsuccessfully):

Repeat: 'Peti*u* oudaril Vasia' ('Petia was hit by Vasia')
Yura: 'Peti*a* oudaril Vasia'
Repeat: 'Vasi*u* oudaril Petia'
Yura: 'Vasi*a* oudaril Petia'
Repeat: 'Petia oudaril Vasi*u*' ('Petia hit Vasia')
Yura: 'Petia oudaril Vasi*u*.'

Twin B

1. A sentence with a simple grammatical construction is easily understood. But a sentence with an inverted (passive) construction is not correctly understood.

2. The repetition of both types of phrase does not show substantial differences; in both cases the subject repeats the phrase as a simple, active one, not noticing that the placing of the words and the relations of inflections are dissimilar in either case.

All this material permits a clear deduction as to the factors which assist development of the processes of speech.

The essential moment, which calls forth the development of speech, is undoubtedly the creation of an objective necessity for speech communication.

Our observations showed that it was only necessary to remove the 'twin situation', in which direct communication without utilization of a language system was sufficient, and to place the children in a normal situation which compelled full-value communication with the aid of speech; for elementary speech interlocked with action, to be very quickly converted into full-value speech activity using a language system and sufficiently clearly separated from direct action. The nature of the subjects, in whom retardation in speech formation was complicated by the twin situation which hindered speech development, provided the opportunity to establish these conclusions reliably.

Our experiment showed that special speech training was not the only decisive factor in the development of the twins' speech activity. This appeared as an independent means of communication as a result of the new objective situation created when our twins were separated. This situation gave rise to a need for verbal speech and became the most significant factor in its development. Special speech training, which made speech an object of conscious perception, accelerated the conscious application of speech and helped the child to acquire an extended grammatical structure of speech; nevertheless, it is clear that this special training played only a subsidiary role, leaving the leading place to the formative influence of direct speech communication.

Chapter 6
Structure of the Mental Processes in Twins G

We have described the peculiar characteristics of the twins' speech during the preliminary period of observation. The question naturally arises: was the primitive character of speech, which was not excluded from action, connected with peculiarities in other mental activities? Could we assume that this primitive speech was connected not only with peculiar forms of communication but also with peculiar attributes in the whole mental life of these children?

Amorphous speech, not excluded from direct activity, is proper to the normal child of one and a half to two years of age. At this stage, because of the incomplete development of neurodynamic processes and the still very elementary forms of life, the child's mental processes are not fully developed. But we observed in our twins a clearly expressed form of this primitive speech at a much later age, from five to five and a half years. At this period the development of neurodynamic processes and of the child's forms of life has naturally moved far ahead and this provided an adequate basis for supposing that there were peculiarities in the twins' activity closely connected with the retardation of their speech which (as has already been indicated) was by no means to be explained in terms of their general 'mental backwardness'. If the rapid improvements in the children's speech communication called forth by our experiment were accompanied by similar significant improvements in the organization of their mental processes, then the relation of the organization of mental processes to the level of development of speech would have been experimentally proved.

We may now attempt to give an analysis of the peculiarities of our twins' mental life, in order thoroughly to investigate the changes in mental life called forth by the experiment.

Play activity

Both twins, when they entered into relation with other children in a situation where we could study them carefully, were sufficiently lively and mobile; they were always very active, looked after themselves very well, carried out the usual tasks of children on duty in the kindergarten, were musical and took part satisfactorily in rhythmic exercises. Their performance of simple practical tasks was no worse than that of the other children. But careful observation brought to light notable differences in the construction of their activity by comparison with their counterparts of the same age. Such differences were, perhaps, most prominent in their play activity.

The researches of Vigotsky, Elkonin, Fradkina and others have shown that it is precisely during the play of children of pre-school age, when their behaviour becomes subordinated to an imaginative pattern, that there appear those peculiar features of activity which give promise of future development, which lay the foundation for a transition to new, more complex forms of mental life.

The child of two and a half to three years is able, in the course of play, to attach to an object some conditional meaning which varies in the process of manipulation. At five to six years the child is in a position to develop complex, subjective play which stems from a definite project; this has the character of an original, active narrative in which the child begins to act a corresponding role which he retains to the end of the game and which determines his behaviour throughout the period of play. Research has shown that an imaginative situation created with the aid of the verbal system can be so stable that casual external factors cannot destroy the system of connections that the child has created with the aid of his speech.

The question arises: to what extent is this complex, meaningful play activity actually connected with the development of speech, which enables the child to proceed to complex connections, characteristic of the 'second signal system', and to build up his activities on their foundation? For an answer to this question we may turn to the data obtained during the observation of our children.

The first records, which were upheld by later material, established that our children's play activity, which reflected the whole organization of their mental life, showed peculiarities which sharply differentiated it from the play of their counterparts. *Primitive play, during which a conditional meaning was created for an object, was completely accessible to our twins. But complex meaningful play, which proceeded from some preliminary project and involved the steady unfolding of this project in a series of play activities, was inaccessible to them.* This was the character of our children's play during the period (from five to five and a half years) of our preliminary investigations.

Observation of their customary play clearly established these facts. As has already been noted, the children readily played with each other for a long time, often attaching conditional meanings to objects (for instance, converting a brick into a cart, a board into a wheelbarrow or a horse etc.). But such play did not as a rule transcend the bounds of primitive, manipulative play with the conditionally determined object; it never proceeded farther to the unfolding of some kind of meaningful play which required the children to fill a specific role and revealed a comprehensible content.

The following extracts are based on our records of the children's behaviour during this period.

Observation 1

The children are playing at horses in a stereotyped way. One of them fills the part of the owner of the horse (he rides on it, feeds it, strokes it, ties it to the chair); the other plays the role of the horse itself, tramples, shouts and pretends to eat hay.

The children play at trams or trains in the same way; they put chairs in a row, sit on them and shout 'ou-ou', 'tou-tou' or 'tin-tin' and fall to the ground.

Such games are repeated many times but do not constitute part of any general plan.

Observation 2

Liosha and Yura are in the playroom. There are several mobile toys before them (engines, tanks, carts), three stools and cubes. Yura has tied an engine to an overturned stool and is pulling at it.

Then he takes a second engine, ties it to the other end of the same stool and calls Liosha: 'En, Liosia, masina, Liosia' (for mashina, engine).

Liosha is sitting near a boy, Alick, who is playing; he does not turn round at Yura's call but continues with his own affairs.

Yura runs towards him, goes up to the box in which they keep their large building materials, takes out several cubes and puts these on a stool.

Yura sits a doll on the stool. Liosha is now sitting in the box and throws out some cubes. Yura places a second row of cubes on the stool. Not finding any more similar cubes he goes away.

He is already playing without the previous interest, glancing either at a cart or at Liosha who continues to sit in the box. Two of the other children come up to the stool and sit on top of the cubes.

Liosha jumps out of the box, comes running up and shouts: 'Liulia!' Yura runs up and shouts to Liosha: 'Liosha, let's go'. They twice carry the stool back and forth across the room. Then they carry it to the box and pile on more cubes. Once more they carry the stool.

Liosha runs out into the corridor, finds a car and brings it. Yura runs behind him, then returns and silently begins carrying the stool; he shouts 'ou-ou'. Liosha carries the car from the table to the corner. Yura again carries the stool to the box and empties the cubes on it into the pile.

Another boy, Iliusha, runs up to them, takes the stool, carries it away and throws it down. Liosha runs to the stool, brings it once more to the brick box and begins to put cubes on it. Yura leaves the car and helps him. They pick up all the cubes from the floor and put them on the stool.

Liosha seats himself in the front. Yura pushes the stool from behind, he shouts: 'Tavai!' ('Davai', 'let's go'). Liosha imitates a gesture of taking up reins, he shouts: 'Tpr!' Yura begins to push the stool.

The same kind of play goes on. The children carry the stool across the room, once more throw the bricks away and then pick them up and put them on the stool. The play continues.

These records indicate that the play of our twins differed sharply from that of their counterparts. The normal child of five to six years old transcends the bounds of the directly perceived situation, his actions are subordinated to imagination and he can create a relatively complex project in play. It was precisely this that remained inaccessible to our twins; in their play they were subordinated to such an extent to connections directly called forth by perceived objects that each object called forth several direct actions and play consisted of a repetition of stereotyped reactions.

Analysis of the imitative play of our twins led to the same conclusions.

Research concerned with the pre-school child has shown that imitative actions reveal particularly clearly tendencies towards further development. The child, when imitatively entering into a complex situation, is able to imitate actions which he cannot yet accomplish independently; and it is as a result of his inclusion in this way in more complex forms of activity that he is able to pass on to the stage of acquiring these actions independently.

It is particularly interesting, therefore, to discover the extent to which our children could imaginatively take part in complex forms of meaningful play which they were unable to master independently at this period.

Our observations showed that the twins quite often took part in collective games. Once the child collective started mobile play (dancing, chasing and catching, mock fights) our twins immediately joined in. But their participation did not depass the limits of affective participation in a common game, in common mobile activity; the significance of the play, any allocation of roles, the rules of a game, these remained entirely inaccessible to our children. They were drawn into the external, ritual side of play activity but remained outside the meaningful aspect.

Several examples may be given to illustrate this.

Both twins readily take part in rhythmic exercises; readily run about with the other children or play at school (not, of course, filling any role in this game but rather participating in direct actions connected with it).

But they never participate in play involving fixed rules; thus they have often watched the game of lotto but each time have gone away without taking part. When they were given lotto and the necessary explanations were made,* they mechanically laid out and relaid the pictures but did not proceed any further.

A typical example of external, ritual imitation of a game was their play with forfeits. The twins had often seen how the other children played, throwing up the forfeits and winning the picture on which one fell. Today, after looking on, they began to play themselves. As has been noted, in imitative play the twins never reproduced the intention but only the external process; therefore in this case, when the game itself had a manipulative character, their imitation produced results which did not differ from the norm and their participation in general play became possible.

On the other hand, when external actions in play covered some kind of conditional meaning or rule, imitation became impossible and the twins dropped out from the play of their counterparts.

Consequently the primitive character of the twins' activity was manifested not only in their independent activity but also in their imitative activity; analysis of this showed that complex intellectual forms of communication were almost inaccessible to them.

This goes a long way towards explaining why their prolonged participation in the collective (up to the time of their separation) did not result in so much improvement in their behaviour as might have been expected.

The limitations of the twins' understanding of meaningful play activity were most clearly revealed in special experiments designed to analyse the extent to which they could attach conditional meanings to objects.

Utilizing a method initiated by Vigotsky, we offered several objects to our twins which were to acquire a conditional meaning in play; thus a penholder acquired the meaning 'papa', a pencil 'mama', a wooden ring 'the house', a box 'the tramcar', an ashtray 'work'. Using the corresponding objects we played out the following project: 'papa travelled to work in the tram'.

The experiment showed that our children easily understood

*As played in the kindergarten, a game with cards bearing different pictures, which are dealt out, and a board with corresponding pictures on it. One child calls the name of the picture and the holder of the card designated lays it on the corresponding picture on the board. [Ed.]

both the agreed meaning of the object and, too, any change in meaning indicated by a gesture. Thus, when the experimenter took a small metal spoon and imitated chopping movements with it, the children, asked what this was, answered 'an axe'. When the experimenter picked up a knife and pretended to sweep the floor, the children at once said 'a brush'.

This proved that where there was manipulation of objects the significance of an object could easily be changed. That a transposition of this kind should be so simply effected is easily understood when it is recalled that the children's own speech was not yet detached from direct activity. Nevertheless, our observations very quickly revealed the limitations to their application of conditional meanings. It was only necessary to separate the meaning verbally attached to an object from direct action for the children to be unable to master it and to show a tendency to resist in order to remain in the sphere of the visual practical situation.

Thus, when the experimenter gave the children a penknife and, not having peformed any action with it, told them that this was a brush, the twins took the knife and, ignoring the verbal indication, began to sharpen a pencil with it. Now, even if the experimenter demonstrated the conditional action of sweeping with the knife, and then passed it to one of the twins with the words 'Take this brush and sweep', Liosha (or in other experiments Yura) took the knife, looking altogether perplexed, glanced at the experimenter and began again to sharpen the pencil.

Thus, *though they could acquire the conditional meaning of an object in the process of concrete activity, our twins were unable to perceive this meaning when it was given to them verbally*, nor could they actively develop the activity determined by that verbal meaning. The experiment showed that they were unable adequately to refer to a verbal indication; when the experimenter said 'Shall this be a brush?' both twins shook their heads negatively and when the question was repeated answered 'it's a knife'.

Though, therefore, *they could easily be included in a visual play situation, our children were unable, either independently or according to an adult's verbal indication, to change a meaning and to retain this changed meaning.*

Peculiarities of constructive activity

The peculiarities characterizing the speech of both twins, its inseparability from action, inevitably implied that they were not in a position to formulate a project such as would determine the direction of their constructive activity. This explains why we did not note any consistent constructive activity during the preliminary period of observation. *In cases when the situation demanded that the children act in accordance with some project, that they realize this project in some developing constructive activity, their actions did not depass the limits of helpless manipulation of objects and there was failure.*

During this period we did not observe even primitive drawing. When we gave the children a sheet of paper and a pencil, or attempted to encourage them to imitate other children drawing, our twins limited themselves to simple scribbling which did not represent anything at all. The children themselves did not name their drawings; they rejected several titles proposed by the experimenter and even when pressed to agree that a designation of some detail was correct they at once rejected this designation.

Similarly, constructional activity with building materials was inaccessible to the twins. When it was suggested that they build something with small building bricks, a simple task for a five year old, our twins were unable to comply; in their case the process of building according to some plan was reduced to casual laying out of any separate cubes which lay handy. The following observations illustrate this.

An experiment with Yura (A)

Yura is at the table; before him are several boxes with cubes of different sizes. The experimenter suggests that he build something with them.

Yura is silent for a long time, then puts a cube from the nearest box on to the table. Still silent. Takes a second similar cube, places it by the first. Takes a small board, which is sometimes in the brick box, holds it in his hands. The experimenter persuades and encourages him for a considerable time. Yura is silent.

An experiment with Liosha (B)

Same situation. Liosha has a finger in his mouth, smiles confusedly. In a moment, takes a cube from the nearest box and places it on the table; takes out the next one and places it beside the first; he pays no attention to other cubes.

Lays out a row of cubes in a stereotyped way. Changes the position of one of the cubes in the row to horizontal, then does the same with the symmetrical cube at the other end of the row. Moves the horizontal cube to a sloping position and continues the row, placing cubes like a radius; around them is laid out the outline of a circle. The result is a design made up of equivalent cubes. When asked what this is, he replies: 'A house'.

While a plan which could determine further constructive activity remained inaccessible to the twins, it is obvious that external 'indirect factors' easily 'mixed in with' their constructive activity and directed the course of their actions.

Thus when it was suggested that they build something with small bricks, while at the same time some large circular boards were left lying on the table, our children were easily influenced to replace constructive activity by simple laying out of single cubes along the outlines of these circles; thus the verbally designated task was replaced by elementary activity, subordinated to external, directly perceived factors.

The following are typical examples of such operations.

Experiment in executing a construction with bricks

On the table is a box of cubes. Beside it an overturned lid with a picture on it. It is suggested to the children that they build something with the cubes.

Liosha (B) turns the lid over and begins to lay cubes on top of the picture. At the same time Yura (A) lays out cubes along the edges of the lid, selecting them according to their thickness.

Liosha, glancing at Yura, also begins to lay cubes in the lid. Selects cubes corresponding in thickness to the depth of the lid, sometimes putting two thin cubes together for this purpose. When he runs short of cubes, shows dissatisfaction. This process continues for ten minutes.

Experiment with mosaics

The children are given a round board with hollows and a corresponding collection of balls. It is suggested that they lay out some kind of pattern. Both twins begin to fill the holes of the external circle, following the shape of the frame. They have no plan, their action is entirely determined by the structure of the available field. Having filled one circle, the children pass to the next one, filling that too in a stereotyped way. Having filled up all the holes they stop and go away.

A similar helplessness was apparent when they were asked to make a pattern with mosaics. The verbally given task appeared to be inaccessible to the twins and instead of laying out any planned figure, they simply started to lay out one ball after another, following the outlines of the circular board until they had filled in the whole circle.

It will be understood that any kind of constructive activity which involved copying models[24] remained completely inaccessible to our twins. Instead of following the model, they either picked up separate cubes and began to lay them out in a stereotyped way to make a flat pattern, or produced a disorderly pile of cubes. Our investigations proved, therefore, that *constructive activity in accordance with a verbally formulated task was beyond our twins, who could not themselves formulate the task verbally and so provide a reinforcement when the corresponding activity began.*

Peculiarities in intellectual processes

In the light of all that has been said, it is necessary to suppose that the intellectual processes of our twins, in particular the processes of abstraction and generalization (which are known to be closely connected with language), were not established in the same way as those of their counterparts; in other words, that the observed features of their speech development had led to a peculiar retardation of all the intellectual processes connected with speech, in particular the processes of abstraction and generalization.

We may illustrate these points from records relating to the operation of classifying objects; an activity which, as we established by control experiments, was completely accessible to the normal child of five to five and a half years.

The children were required to single out one object from among a variety of objects (toy animals, wagons, engines, plates etc.), then each child had to select other 'appropriate objects' to make up some unitary group. The kindergarten children of five to six years easily accomplished the task of uniting objects into groups; they usually reproduced some kind of concrete situation–'a school', 'a street', 'a kitchen' – or else generalized objects according to some common feature – made of iron, made of wood, animals etc.

The twins, however, though they could easily correlate objects in the course of concrete activity, were entirely unable to systematize them, to unite them in separate groups; the very process of classification, primitive though it is, remained entirely inaccessible to them.

As a rule, instead of *classifying* the objects, our children merely began to *range them* together one after another, either playing some kind of game or setting them out inconsistently along the edges of the table.

These experiments contribute important material for analysis of the construction of the twins' intellectual processes. Their activity as a whole is determined by the fact that *the process of correlation of objects arises only in the course of direct action*; it does not yet exist as an independent operation of generalization, isolated from action and realized according to the abstract categories provided by a language system. An operation which the normal child of this age can easily accomplish with the aid of speech, the generalization of objects according to concrete similarities, was inaccessible to our children. Their speech itself, since it was not separated from action, could neither generalize the objects nor organize and direct activity. In other words, the operation of attributing objects to certain categories, the task of classification, which is realized on the foundation of 'a new principle of nervous activity' – abstraction and generalization – was impossible for our children. To their primitive speech, interlocked with action, corresponded a primitive organization of activity subordinated to direct action.

Chapter 7
Variations in the Structure of Mental Activity in Twins G with the Development of Speech

We have described those peculiarities in the organization of the twins' mental activity which were integrally connected with the elementary character of their speech processes. Since their speech was not yet singled out from direct activity it could not fix a verbal project, could not give to their activities a steady, goal-directed character and so subordinate them to a specific internal plan. It is clear, then, that the radical improvements in the twins' speech activity called forth by our experiment could not but be reflected in the whole structure of their mental processes.

With the appearance of speech disconnected from action, indicating an object, actions and relations, it was to be expected that there should also arise *the possibility of formulating a system of connections transcending the boundaries of the immediate situation* and *of subordinating action to these verbally formulated connections.* It was to be expected that this would also lead to the development of complex forms of activity, manifested in play as 'the unfolding of subject matter' which would give play a steady character. Finally, such a reorganization of mental processes under the influence of developing speech could be expected to change the child's attitude to the product of activity; that is, by comparison of the result obtained during the process of activity with that system of connections which underlay the project, the child ought to reach a position where he could objectively evaluate this product apart from his activity and consequently also take up a critical relation to it.

In other words, we had every reason to suppose that the acquisition of language would introduce important new peculiarities in the structure of our children's mental processes.

The observations recorded during the experiment proved this general hypothesis.

A check carried out three months after the twins were separated showed how great was the progress both had made during this short time. We may give here a brief analysis of the changes observed in their mental processes in the course of play and in the performance of special intellectual tasks.

Improvements in play activity

It has been noted that before the experiment both twins were usually excluded from general meaningful play engaged in by the children of their group. Three months after the experiment began the position had sharply changed. Both twins, having been placed in different groups of the kindergarten, were less cut off from the general play activities of the other children. Their play clearly revealed elements which far surpassed the very simple manipulations that had formerly been characteristic. We may give here a record illustrating the type of play characteristic of both children after three months of the experiment. For the purposes of comparative observation the twins were placed together, though they were usually in different groups.*

The twins are in the playroom; before them are several play materials analogous to those used during the preliminary observation.

The children take a stool. Yura (A): 'I'm the driver.' Liosha (B): 'Now Liulia engine, Liosia driver'. Yura points at the brick box: 'To build a house.' Liosha, turning to the instructor: 'May we have cubes?' Getting permission, takes these.

The instructor removes a flower which was on the box. Liosha: 'Where's the flower?' Loads cubes on the stool. Yura points out where he should carry them: 'Go there.' Liosha carries the stool. Yura stands up performing an action like a railway signal: 'Stop, oi.' Liosha, sitting, makes a noise like a horn.

Yura takes cubes from the box and making a noise throws them on the stool. Instructor: 'What are you doing Yura?' Yura: 'Laying cubes. Now it's good, a good house, but Liosha isn't. Liosha no make house.'

Instructor: 'What is Liosha going to do?' Yura: 'Drive away.'

Liosha, carrying cubes, stops, says: 'Heavy.' Carries the box going

*In this and the following examples faulty pronunciation must be assumed. [Ed.]

along on his knees; Yura points out the direction, lifting his arms like a railway signal. Liosha stops. They carry the cubes to the opposite corner of the room. Liosha sits on the floor. Yura: 'Now I know, the metropolitan.'

Liosha is sitting on the floor. Liosha: 'Show me.' Yura points in a lively way. Then, turning to Liosha, says: 'Liosha carries cubes.' Begins to build a house. Liosha sits, observes and sometimes makes remarks.

Yura follows the plan he has adopted. 'Now I made dark-dark, how it was, remember?' He puts on more cubes and looks inside. 'Dark. No.' Liosha: 'A bit dark (here he corrects himself) a little bit dark, we must do some more.' Begins to help Yura to build: 'How dark.' Yura looks and says: 'Dark, look.'

Shows Liosha where to go for cubes. Yura: 'Now there's still the circle there.' Liosha gets to his feet, whistles and they go off. He goes in a circle, Yura after him. They arrive at the place, sit down and load on cubes. Afterwards they again convey them to the spot and continue their building, checking to see that the inside is dark.

First, what sharply distinguishes this play from similar play described earlier is the abundance of speech which was formerly absent. Evidently this difference was not merely external. Complex speech, with which the twins now began to accompany their play, fulfils an essential function; from the outset it is a form of the child's orienting activity, bears the character of analysis of the play situation and realization of the play project which is developed through a complex unfolding of several stages of the subject matter of play.

From the outset the children single out a project and they formulate it verbally; this project falls into several stages (loading up and transporting the cubes, building and then additional carting); these different stages are reflected in speech which singles things out, fixes the play situation and plans the succeeding activity; the play gestures cease to be ritual and acquire an objective, indicatory character (for instance, 'signalling', which one of the subjects performed twice).

Separate objects are not merely used in this or that process of play, but take on a permanent significance in its context. What is particularly important here is that this meaning is retained during the whole period of play; the meaning arises not from direct action, but from a verbal formulation of the project ('metropolitan', 'dark inside' etc.); there appears a relation to the product of play (evaluation, checking of how the project is fulfilled); in short, the whole process is radically changed, and play, from being a ritual, becomes fully objective and meaningful.

In the last analysis this meant that the children were now in a position to *detach themselves from the immediate situation, to subordinate their activity to a verbally formulated project* and so *to stand in a new relation to this situation*. It is characteristic that this improvement appeared in both twins, and this permits us to deduce that it was connected with the objective notional speech which arose in them at this period.

Improvements in constructive activity

If substantial improvements were registered in the conduct of free play, constructive activity showed even greater improvement.

Formerly, as has been shown, any kind of real constructive activity was inaccessible to our twins. Now that the children were in a position not only to exclaim and to apply separate meanings arising during the course of activity, but also objectively to formulate their projects, productive activity began to be possible. This took place according to the clear phases of a verbally formulated project, preparation of activity and its realization; now the product of activity 'already existed in the imagination . . . at the commencement'* and it was precisely this that created entirely different relations to the process of creation and its entirely different end product.

We began with observations of modelling and drawing. Neither of these processes was accessible to our twins during the first period of observation; now both these activities flowed differently.

*The reference is to Marx: 'A bee puts to shame many an architect in the construction of her cells. But what distinguishes the worst architect from the best of bees is this, that the architect raises his structure in imagination before he erects it in reality. At the end of every labour-process, we get a result that already existed in the imagination of the labourer at the commencement' in Dona Torr (ed.) (*Capital*, London, 1946, p. 157 – Ed.).

The children are given plasticine; they are separated from each other by a screen. It is suggested to them that they model something; they are told not to talk to each other. Yura (A) is unable to stop talking, Liosha (B) is silent, nevertheless he always reacts to Yura's words.

Yura: 'I'll do a house.'

Liosha: 'And I a sausage. Liosha can do a house.' The instructor reminds the children that they are not to talk to each other.

Yura: 'I want to talk.'

Liosha: 'Liosha a sausage (he laughs) Liosha's talking.'

Yura: 'Aga, he said' – here he continues to talk aloud to himself about what he is doing – 'now one more little leg.'

Liosha, having heard this, also begins to make a table; looks at the table in front of him and, passing his hand round the four edges says: 'So-so-so-so' and begins to model.

Yura: 'Now a leg, I've finished the table.' Both finish making a table. There result certain objects; Yura's is the better, more differentiated (a table with four legs) and Liosha's more primitive (a table with two legs).

Yura continues to hold the plasticine. 'What else? A carrot'. He models a small carrot. He makes the ends so that it looks like a bottle. 'Now I have a good bottle. Liosha can't do a carrot.'

Liosha: 'He can.'

Yura: 'A bottle. But can you do a bottle?'

He plays with the things he has made; the bottle stands up, the carrot lies beside it. 'Now I'll put the carrot here.' The play continues.

The children make sausages, biscuits, little boys, they play with these. When the plasticine is finished Yura says: 'Give me more clay. I'm good . . .' – at modelling.

Completely analagous improvements were observed in the children's drawings. Instead of scribbles there appeared goal-directed, differentiated, objective drawing.

It is characteristic that this basic improvement – from elementary manipulation of materials and meaningless scribbling with a pencil to drawing activity of an objective character – occurred in both twins and reflected the ability verbally to formulate projects which was formed in both children at this period.

This process of formulating a project was most clearly to be observed in another operation – the cutting out of paper shapes. The following passages from our records clearly illustrate this.

The children are cutting out paper shapes. Yura (A) joins them, cuts out a figure: 'I have a fish . . . now eyes.' Takes a pencil, draws eyes for the fish. Tries to stick the drawing, dirties it, starts to cut out a new one. Produces a figure. 'Here's a fish, what a mouth'.

Noticing Vasia's fir tree: 'Now me too.' Begins to cut out, cuts out a figure: 'Like in Vasia's book.' Cuts up its edges, says again: 'A fish.' Cuts off a part of the drawing which is stuck on and says: 'A little candle.' The remaining part is stuck on in the same way: 'This is a bottle.'

The teacher shows the children the work of one of them and says: 'Look at this house, children, it even has a flag.' Yura at once takes the scissors in order to cut out a flag.

One of the boys calls him to come and build a house. Yura, continuing to cut out, answers: 'Soon'; continues to cut out a flag; the flag breaks. Yura begins to cut out a new one, the boy again comes up and calls him. Yura does not answer. Continuing to cut out says: 'Here's a flag. Now I'll cut out another flag.' Starts to work again.

These extracts show that all the child's actions bear the character of intelligent realization of a project, one which, once formed, begins to subordinate the child's further activity.

Now that the twins' activity began to be determined by a project formulated in speech, they were capable of resisting occasional external influences and of realizing their project independently of these irrelevant influences. This can be illustrated by an experiment in laying out mosaics.

As has been shown above, this process was not accessible to the children during the preliminary period of observation; their activity was limited to the passive laying out of mosaics along the outline of the given form. Now this activity gradually became possible. This is how it proceeded, in the case of both twins, three months after the experiment began.

Yura (A) takes the board and from the outset lays out red balls round the outside, then, filling in one contour of the board with brown balls, a second with white and a third with red, says: 'Look what a boat I have, now I'll make a flag.'

This process differs greatly from the meaningless laying out of balls along the outlines of the board; the vector of the external 'field' has ceased to play any role.

Same situation. Takes the board, begins by laying out radial outlines; afterwards fills in each sector with balls of different colours. Asks
whether he has done it well. Asked what it is, answers: 'A little circle.'

After this puts the balls in the box and says: 'Now a boat.' Begins to
make a new figure, says: 'Look at this.'

The constancy of the verbal project and the independence of
action from accessory external influences indicate the radical
improvements which had taken place in the twins' mental activity
at this time.

It remains to note two final moments which were already
established a few months after the experiment began and which
appeared to be extremely characteristic: that is, *the stability of
productive activity* on the one hand and *the children's active attitude to the product of this activity* on the other.

Observations carried out during the preliminary period showed
that it was usually very easy to divert both twins from their
primitive play activity which had no defined subject matter. They
easily switched over to some other activity, leaving the game they
had started, and did not independently take up the discarded
activity again. There did not arise that 'mental tension' which
was characteristic of the meaningful play activity of their counterparts.

It was precisely this peculiarity that changed radically during
the first months of the experiment. Passing over to developed,
complex, meaningful play, our twins were not only in a position
to develop this in adequately complex forms but also revealed a
tendency to return permanently to a previous activity. Now it was
no longer easy to distract them from meaningful play and they
did not easily leave their play as before.

Here is an illustration of this

In the evening Yura was busy building a 'metro'. He carried the cubes,
built a 'station' and a 'tunnel'. According to the teacher on duty, he
took a long time to go to sleep, contrary to his usual habit – 'he was
thinking all the time about the metro'.

The next day he returned to this building first thing in the morning.
He sharply protested when his partner in play proposed demolishing
the construction. 'Why knock it down, I want to play,' and continued

to build. When any of the other children tried to take some cubes, he took them back, restored the building and returned to playing with it.

This extract from our records demonstrates that complex and meaningful play, making use of stable objects, brings to life new forms of affective relations, which acquire the character of a steady tension continuing throughout the period that the verbally formulated objective activity continues.

Similar significant improvements were observed in the children's attitude to the product of their activity.

During the preliminary period of observation our twins easily passed from one form of manipulation of objects to another, thereby revealing that they did not have any evaluatory attitude to the forms of objective organization of play. Now this attitude radically changed and the children began to compare the product of activity with the original project, to evaluate it, and, where possible, to improve on it. Here are examples of such evaluation.

Yura (A) watching how other children lay out mosaics remarks that they have been laid out wrongly, says: 'No, not that way . . .' and remakes the pattern.

Yura, watching other children drawing, says: 'Bad . . . Bad . . . You make it very bad!'

When cutting out, he is not satisfied with the results of his own work; he begins to cut out another shape. When the experimenter gives him a roughly cut out model, he first smiles, then says: 'Not that way' and cuts out another himself.

This material, taken as a whole, permits us to draw some general conclusions. Only three months after their separation sharp improvements could be observed in the twins' activity. These were expressed in the fact that *the children's attitude to objects began to be seen, not only in the process of direct activity, but also in the form of projects formulated in their own speech* which was now separated from action and in a position to subordinate action. Parallel with this, *play activity also developed* and became differentiated into separate moments which did not have an equivalent significance (project, preparation of the activity, its fulfilment); an objective relation to the product of activity arose; a new system of reinforcement of intellectual activity was formed.

All these improvements took place within a very short period, during which, of course, natural 'maturation' played only an insignificant role but which was marked by the introduction of an important new factor in the shape of a leap forward in speech development. This permits us to deduce that improvements in the productive activity of both twins took place in close connection with the acquisition of a language system which introduced new potentialities for the organization of the child's mental life.

Improvements in intellectual operations: the appearance of inter-pair differences

The facts outlined point clearly to significant psychological improvements in both twins as a result of their inclusion in new forms of speech communication and in connection with the acquisition of an objective language system. It only remains to throw light on one final question; what influence did the special training in speech, undergone by one of our twins, have on development? We may deal with this question by analysing the intellectual operations which showed the greater degree of improvement in relation to this training.

As has been shown earlier, the separation of the twins was accompanied by an essential supplementary factor; one of them (Twin A) was given systematic exercises during which he was specifically trained to speak. These lessons have been described; they took the form of dialogue conversations, verbal analysis of pictures, the relating of stories.

Did these supplementary lessons give rise to special improvements in the twin who received speech training? Did he differ in any way from the second twin who was not trained in speech?

Observations undertaken three months after the experiment began showed that notable inter-pair differences had arisen which had had no place before.

As has been pointed out, up to the time of separation Yura (Twin A) was the weaker, Liosha (Twin B) the more active. It is only necessary to analyse the extracts given above, from records of the play of both twins, to be convinced that the position has been reversed. Now the trained twin Yura (Twin A) began to take a more and more leading part; as regards speech activity he greatly surpassed his twin brother; in play he never let the initiative out of his hands, first formulating the project and then taking the active role, while Twin B only followed him. It is characteristic that such a change of roles only appeared in those forms of intellectual activity connected with verbal formulation of a project; in mobile games, in running, in motor activity in general, we were unable to observe any such difference; here, as before, Liosha (Twin B) retained the superiority.

Steady and clear inter-pair differences could be observed in the peculiarities of operations realized with the aid of speech.

As has been shown above, significant improvements in these operations were recorded for both twins; nevertheless, notable inter-pair intellectual differences came to the fore. These were clearly shown in special play which involved attaching a conditional meaning to things, as well as in the creation of a play situation already described above.

This is demonstrated in the records of an experiment in deciphering and active organization of play which involved attaching conditional meanings to objects. This was undertaken after ten months of the experiment.

Both children are asked to play out several examples of a game which involves attaching conditional meanings to objects. They are told that the pencil is 'mama'; the vase, 'a tree'; the spoon, 'a wolf' etc. The game, which comprises subject matter covering corresponding things, is played out with the aid of the objects.

The differences between the twins are here very substantial.

Twin A deciphers the meaning of the gesture game at once, during manipulation of objects; decoding does not present any difficulties to him and he immediately describes the whole game verbally: 'The engine drives along, the mother wolf runs, the little wolf goes up the tree, mama comes out of the house, sits on the engine, takes the boy' etc.

When asked to make up a game independently with the same objects, does this easily; some of the conditional meanings are retained, others created anew. 'Mama caught a hare, the wolf ran to look for the hare, the engine drove along, the hare was in the house with mama, it jumped through the window straight onto the fir-tree ...'

The same operation was performed altogether differently by Twin B who had not undergone speech training.

He could not decode the stories related by gestures immediately but was only able to do this in parts and then only in reply to questions put to him. When asked to repeat the game, he repeated it without any changes, as it had been shown to him by gestures, and when asked to give new meanings to the objects he refused.

The clear differences revealed here – in relation to deciphering the meaning of a game and, what is more important, to developing it and operating freely with new verbal meanings – must be attributed to the special training in speech of one of the twins.

Further significant differences appeared in the comprehension or perception of speech.

These were demonstrated when, after ten months of the experiment, a simple story was read to the children and they were asked to relate its content. Twin A, who had undergone speech training, began to relate the story adding supplementary points in answer to questions; but Twin B did not relate the story on his own initiative, saying that he had forgotten it, and only reproduced details in the course of subsequent dialogue.

Similar divergences appeared when pictures were described. An example may be given which shows significant differences between the twins in verbal reproduction.

Both children are given a picture representing a mother and a girl at the table; a cat is sitting on the floor near them.

Yura (Twin A)

('Devochka plachet. Kiska lezhit. Mama sela na toul (stoul). Na tsole (stole) tsoit (stoit) hleb. Kolevat (krovat) na polu tsoit. Na tsole hleb.')
'The girl is crying. The cat lies down. Mama sat at the table. The bread is standing on the table. The bed is standing on the floor. The bread is on the table.'

The question is put to him: 'Why is the girl crying?'

Yura: 'The cat scratches.'

'With what?'

Yura: 'With paws.'

'Why?'

Yura: 'Doesn't give milk.'

Liosha (Twin B)

('Kiska. Devochka. Mama. Kaliavat (krovat). Okino (okno). Talelka (tarelka). Piliagi (pirogi). Iatsik (iashchik). Tsol (stol)'.)

'The cat. The girl. Mama. A bed. A window. A plate. Cakes. A box. A table.'
The question is put to him: 'What is the girl doing?'
Liosha: 'She's crying.'
'What for?'
Liosha: 'Don't know, she wants a drink.'

The children are given a picture representing a storm at sea and a boat with people in it fighting the waves.

Yura (Twin A)
('Plavaet na lodi. Palkami lipki (rybki) loviat. Devochka sidit c mamoi. Paliahody (parohody) ezdiiut. Chemodan tsoit (stoit).')
'Float in the boat. Catch fish with the stick. The girl sits with mama. The ships are sailing. The trunk stands up.'

Liosha (Twin B)
('Na lodke kataiutsia. Chemodany. Diadenka. Devochki. Mole (more).')
'They ride in the boat. The trunks. An uncle. Girls. The sea.'
To separate questions about the meaning of the picture answers: 'Don't know.'
These records show how clear the differences now were in the children's speech activity.

The first twin gives, as a rule, a sufficiently developed judgement, describing separate actions represented in the picture. But the untrained Twin B, in his descriptions of a picture, remains within the bounds of the denotary function of speech and does not make the transition to independent description of the subject.

This difference between the twins was most clearly demonstrated in their ability to analyse the component parts of a drawing.

In order to discover peculiarities in visual analysis, both children were given drawings with several deficiencies (a man without a nose, an ear, a hand etc.) or drawings in which some of the details were obviously absurd.

Analysis of their answers shows that Twin A quickly detected absurdities in a drawing, quickly pointed out what was missing in the drawing of the man, or formulated in speech what he rgarded as wrong with a drawing as a whole. On the other hand the untrained Twin B singled out faults with significantly greater strain, and it was impossible to make sure whether he saw only the defect in some outline or the defective meaning of a drawing as a whole, because he did not single out the place of the defect and only evaluated a drawing as incorrect after detailed questioning.

All this demonstrates that speech analysis of perceived material became notably different in either child and that the substantial role in determining these differences was played by the special training in speech of one of them.

The inter-pair differences observed were not limited to the processes of visual analysis; they were particularly clearly disclosed in the case of intellectual operations, above all the operation of classification.

During the preliminary observations, the operation of classifying objects was entirely inaccessible to both twins; neither depassed the limits of simple setting out of the objects. But after ten months of the experiment this operation was accessible to both children. Both readily took part in this task, formulated it in speech, chose objects which resembled each other and placed them in corresponding groups in accordance with a definite aim. Nevertheless clear differences were observed both in the manner of selection and in the structure of the groups of objects formed, showing once more the divergence between the twins as a result of the special training of one.

Extracts from the relevant records indicate these differences, in relation to the task of classifying pictures.

Yura (A)

For a long time does not begin to assemble pictures himself. The experimenter shows a blue flower.

'What goes with this?' Yura is silent. Experimenter (taking a picture of socks): 'Do these go?' – 'No.' 'Or these?' (some other flowers) – 'They will go.'

Then Yura is silent for a long time and finally places a picture representing blue trousers.

Experimenter: (giving a red flower): 'Will this go?' Yura nods his head. Experimenter gives a picture of some berries. Yura: 'This is a currant.' Then adds to this a potato, swede, radish, carrot, cucumber, strawberry, raspberry.

Experimenter: 'Will anything else go there?' Yura shakes his head negatively and begins with a new lot of pictures: an aeroplane, bicycle, car, chair, armchair, divan, tramcar, carriage etc. In a final group he places: a shirt, trousers, a cup, a bed, clothes etc.

When checking he makes some things more exact, separating flowers and berries.

Here he hesitates a little about where to place the currant (which according to its colour belongs in the group of flowers) but then places it with the berries.

When the experimenter asks why he placed it in this way, answers 'Because it isn't a flower.'

Liosha (B)

Does not understand the instructions for a long time. The experimenter's example is not perceived; when he puts together a group of flowers, Liosha perceives this purely externally and begins to put together any kind of picture saying (in imitation of the experimenter): 'The knife is like the table, the tramcar is like the carrot,' etc.

Soon colour is singled out as a feature which links pictures different in meaning. An attempt to transfer to meaning as a principle of selection fails. The subject soon slips from selection to collection of different objects.

After four days another experiment takes place. When initial instructions have been given, the subject at once begins to put aside pictures representing a red shirt, red teapot, red tramcar; then, in another group, pictures representing blue socks, a blue flower, several black objects (a bicycle, divan, chair, horse, cat).

When the basis of the classification is checked, it points to colour. The experimenter explains that it is necessary to produce a classification on the basis of meaning. The subject sets aside pictures representing a kettle and a tramcar: 'The kettle is iron and the tramcar.'

However, when asked to what group the hen (which is red) belongs, whether with the white goose or with the raspberry, places it with the raspberry.

In all the subsequent control experiments once more slips into external comparison of objects according to colour.

Here significant differences in the process of classification are clearly demonstrated. In the case of Twin A, the process of selective generalization has a developed, objective character and transcends the limits of direct perception of the objects (their form and colour). But in Twin B this process is determined to a notable degree by the external similarity of the objects, and attempts to introduce generalization depassing the limits of the visual field of perception did not meet with success.

These peculiarities arose still more clearly in the course of a similar experiment with a number of toys.

The twins are given several toys (enumerated in the earlier experiment described above).

Yura (A)

At first places the toys separately, looks at them, puts together identical things. Then places a sailor with a boat. Places next to a lorry a hammer and brush: 'They will mend, they'll paint.' Afterwards places a little pig: 'I saw a cow carried in a car, like this.'

To the engine adds the key – 'they will lock the engine door' – and two nails – 'to make the engine strong.'

Holds a reel of cotton in his hand for a long time, then stands it by the sailor: 'They will sew on buttons that come off.'

To the lorry adds the pencil: 'It will write the number, which is here . . .' Puts with the bear, the hare and two mushrooms: 'The mushrooms are growing in the forest there, the bear sits there and the hare jumps about in the forest.'

There result these groups: 1. Horse, cow, cart, goat, pig, dog, tree. 2. Bear, hare and two mushrooms. 3. Plate and, surrounding it, the hen, chicken, goose. 4. Lorry, two sailors, the shepherd, the button etc.

Liosha (B)

First takes the train, places a car next to it, then, around these a cart, harnesses to this a horse, and adds a goat, chicken, pig and rabbit.

The experimenter repeats the instructions: to divide into appropriate groups. Liosha places 1. the train, car, boat; then separately 2. two dogs; astride one of them a bear; 3. the horse with the cart and a cow; 4. the aeroplane, in which is the figure of a man and the goose; 5. picks up a soup bowl, stands a cup on it and picking out all the crockery says: 'The kitchen.' 6. In half of a dividing ball he puts the reel of cotton, paintbrush, pencil, exercise book, key: 'This is a group' (class). Then relates where the class is held. The experimenter points to the second group: 'And what is this?' – 'A street.' 'And this?' 4. – 'A street.' 'Does the goose go with the aeroplane?' – 'It does.' 'And this?' 1. – 'An engine.' 'Here are a boat and a car, what is it all?' – 'Another street.'

Names other groups he has made in the same way.

The differences already noted are exhibited here particularly clearly. As a rule, when the trained Twin A groups objects he includes them each time in a situation formed with the aid of speech; each object is allocated to the corresponding group he so formulates, and the whole classification takes on the precise, definite character of an operation in 'an imaginative plan'.

Altogether different peculiarities distinguish the process of classification in the case of Twin B. Here the grouping of objects continues to arise only in the process of direct manipulation of these objects, and bears, therefore, a more direct character. Verbal formulation does not arise in the actual process of manipulation but only after this, when the objects have been manipulated, and is, therefore, not so much the foundation as the result of the given manipulation.

In this case, the very grouping of objects itself is accomplished chiefly on the basis of incidental indications; this shows that a verbally formulated project does not determine the whole structure of the intellectual process and the latter is, in an important measure, subordinated to direct relations to objects and to the reproduction of the visual situation with which they are connected.

Specific differences between the twins, appearing as a result of the special speech training of one of them, were also clearly demonstrated in an investigation of elementary operations of discursive thinking.

When, after ten months of the experiment, the twins were asked to find the difference between two objects, they resolved this problem in a different way. Twin A detected a difference between objects, for instance (when comparing the conception of 'a stone' with the conception of 'an egg'): 'A stone is black, an egg is white'. But Twin B usually did not depass the limits of simple description of a single common feature of the situation (e.g. 'a white stone and a white egg') and therefore did not even begin the necessary operation of comparison.

Differences between the twins showed up even more distinctly when it was a question of operations of deduction from verbal premises.

This operation was accessible to the trained Twin A but proved difficult for Twin B. Twin A generalized a single response and drew from it a logical deduction. But Twin B retained the individual response within the limits of the specific facts stated; it did not, therefore, become the prerequisite for a corresponding deduction and was not transformed into reasoning.

We may give a specific example of this.

Both children are presented with pictures comprising a series of absurdities. Here is how reasoning proceeded in the case of either twin.

Yura (A)

'Do you think this happens?' – 'It does.' 'What is the cat doing?' – 'The cat is playing.' 'Can a cat really play on the violin?' – 'No.' 'Then does this happen?' – 'No.'

Liosha (B)

'Is this drawing right?' – 'It is.' 'Can a cat really dance like this?' – 'No.' 'Then is this drawing right or not?' – 'Right.' 'Have you seen a cat play on a balalaika?' – 'No.' 'Then is the drawing right or not?'– 'Right.' 'But can a cat play a balalaika?' etc.

This indicates clearly how great were the differences revealed in the flow of intellectual processes in our twins.

Finally we may examine data indicating essential differences in discursive activity between the twins, arising as a result of the fact that one of them gradually passed through a course of speech training.

We have already pointed out elsewhere[25] that at the early stages of development the child cannot yet perceive a word in itself; that only in the process of play, and further of teaching in school, does the word itself become an object of special perception and special conscious activity.

It is precisely in this respect that differences between the twins were manifested, one having been specially trained in speech while, in the other, speech arose only as a result of practical activity.

When, therefore, after ten months of the experiment, both twins were set problems involving a series of operations with the aid of their own speech, it was demonstrated that an elementary special operation with the aid of speech was accessible to the trained Twin A but remained inaccessible to Twin B who had not undergone special speech training.

Several examples may be given to illustrate this position. The children are given a series of words (at first singly, then in a sentence) and are asked to reckon up these words.

Twin A easily reckons up the words in a sentence and then easily extracts them in order, indicating the second and third words. Twin B cannot extract a separate word, he extracts not a word but only an object or a situation without understanding the words, and cannot master the operation further than this even when we give him the necessary help.

Twin A

'Mama: went: to the shop.* How many words?' – 'Three.' 'The first?' – 'Mama.' 'The second?' – 'went.' 'The third?' – 'the shop.'

'The girl: ate: the cake. How many words here?' – 'Three.' 'The first?' – 'The girl ate the cake.' 'No, the first?' – 'The girl.' 'The second?' – 'ate.' 'The third?' – 'the cake.'

Twin B

'The boy: hit: the dog. How many words?' – 'Two.' 'The first?' – 'The boy.' 'The second?' – 'the dog.'

'The dog: bit: the boy. How many words?' – 'Two.' 'The first?' – 'The boy.' 'The second?' – 'The dog.' 'Are there really two? No more?' (When counting again the subject once more gives two elements.)

After this, though Liosha could correctly extract words from sentences consisting of two elements, he could not do so in relation to sentences with three words.

'The boy: was eating: a sweet. How many words?' – 'Two.' 'The first?' – 'The boy.' 'The second?' – 'a sweet.') Further experiments did not result in a correct solution to the problem.)

When both twins were given sentences including indications of a quantity of objects which differed from the number of words in the sentence, Twin A easily abstracted the quantity from the

*The colons indicate the three Russian words (e.g. 'Mama: poshla: v magazin'). In later examples a literal translation is given to maintain the same order of words. (Ed.)

situation and added up the number of words included in the sentence; but Twin B could not master this abstraction and persisted in adding up the objects mentioned in the sentence.

Twin A

'In the room: (are) five: chairs. How many words here?' – 'Three.' 'The first?' – 'In the room.' 'The second?' – 'five.' 'The third?' – 'chairs.'

Twin B

'In the room: (is) one: chair. How many words here?' – 'One.' 'And – In the dining room: one: girl?' – 'Two.' 'The first?' – 'girl.' 'The second?' – 'the dining room.'

'And – In the dining room: five: girls?' – 'Six.' 'The first?' – 'The dining room.' 'The second?' – 'girls.' 'The third?' – 'Don't know.'

Later the children were given sentences and asked to say whether a particular word had been in them, the word in the question sometimes only being analagous in sense to the original word in the sentence. Twin A could easily identify word from word, mastering the operation of analogy, but Twin B did not succeed in solving this problem.

Twin A

Easily distinguishes a word formerly in a sentence from its synonym. ('Na ulitze idiot sneg') 'In the street: comes: snow. Have I said here the word "snow"?' – 'You have.' 'And "falls" (padaet)?' – 'No.' 'And – "comes" (idiot)?' – 'Yes' etc.

('Malchik koupalsia v vannie') 'The boy: was bathing himself: in the tub. Was the word "boy" here?' – 'Yes.' 'Trough (Koryto)?' – 'No.' 'Was washing himself (mylsia)?' – 'No.' 'Was bathing himself (koupalsia)?' – 'Yes.'

Twin B

There is a tendency to detach the word from the sense and to confuse verb synonyms.

('Malchik koupalsia v vannie') 'The boy: was bathing himself: in the tub. Did I say here the word "boy"?' – 'Yes.' 'Trough (Koryto)?' – 'No.' 'Was washing himself (mylsia)?' – 'You did.' 'Was bathing himself (koupalsia)?' – (a pause) 'You did.'

('Deduschka podaril igrushku') 'Grandfather: gave away: a toy. The word "gave away"?' – 'You said it.' 'Old man (Starichok)?' – 'No.' 'Gave (dal)?' – 'You said it.' 'Ball (Miachik)?' – 'No.'

Our observations brought to light essential differences between the twins as regards capacity to assess the grammatical correct-ness of a sentence. Both twins were given sentences with a grammatically incorrect structure, then asked to assess their correctness and say how the sentence should be corrected. Twin A easily detected the error and in the given conditions was able to correct the sentence. This problem remained entirely inaccessible to Twin B, who was still so deficient in grammar that he could not sense the defect in a sentence and so was unable to correct it.

Twin A
Detects an error in a sentence but cannot at first correct it; later easily masters the problem.
('Ia kushal konfetk*ami*') 'I was eating: with sweets. Did I say that cor-rectly?' The subject repeats the sentence without alteration. Is con-fused.
('Ia risuiu tetradk*ami*') 'I am drawing: *with* an exercise book. Is that right?' – 'No.' 'How must it be said?' – 'I am drawing *in* an exercise book' ('Ia risuiu *na* tetradk*e*').
('Ia liubliu igrushkami?') 'I like: with toys?' – 'Wrong.' 'What is right?' – 'I like to play with toys' ('Ia liubliu igrat igrushkami').

Twin B
Cannot understand mistakes in the construction of a sentence even after they have been explained. In each case assesses an ungrammatical sentence as correct.
('Ia kushal konfetkami') 'I was eating with sweets. Did I say that right?' – 'Right' etc.

The facts given above allow us to point to precise differences between the twins, arising after their separation and accompany-ing the special training of one of them.

After ten months of the experiment both twins developed full-value practical speech activity as a result of which there was a per-ceptible reorganization of their intellectual processes. But only one of them, Twin A who had undergone continuous systematic exercises in speech, developed a '*theoretical attitude*' *towards speech* proper to his age. In the case of this twin, speech became an object of special perceptual activity, its structure was per-ceived, and precisely because of this elementary discursive operations became accessible to him while remaining inaccessible to the other twin.

The appearance of these discursive operations must be attributed to the special training which was undertaken with one of the twins.

Chapter 8
Conclusions

This concludes the survey of the course of our experiment and we may now summarize some of the more essential conclusions.

It is well known to scientific or materialist psychology that speech, which reflects objective reality, directly influences the formation of complex human activity; that the second signal system introduces 'a new principle of nervous activity – the abstraction and with this the generalization' of the preceding signals and thereby raises mental processes to a new level.

As yet, however, insufficient material has been provided to establish, with the necessary precision and on a firm foundation of evidence, the extent to which language exercises this formative influence on mental processes, about which we all know, and with what specific results. The present experiment was designed to throw light on this problem.

We were able to find appropriate subjects, a pair of identical twins of five years of age who suffered from a peculiar defect which created conditions for a retardation of speech development; added to this was the 'twin situation' which did not create an objective necessity for developing language and so constituted a factor which fixed this retardation.

During the preliminary period of our observations, the twins did not experience the necessity of using language to communicate with each other; a self-sufficient pair, they at most experienced the necessity 'to point to something in the process of practical activity', and it was as a result of this situation that they developed elementary 'synpraxic' speech interlocked with action.

This primitive speech did not normally depass the limits of naming objects in the process of direct intercourse and most frequently of all took the form of exclamations which only acquired significance in dependence upon the action of which they formed a part.

To this primitive speech, interlocked with action, there

corresponded a peculiar, insufficiently differentiated, structure of consciousness; as has been shown, the twins were unable to detach the word from action, to master orienting, planning activity, to formulate the aims of activity with the aid of speech and so to subordinate their further activity to this verbal formulation. Therefore, even at the age of five to five and a half years our twins could not master skills nor organize complex play of a kind proper to children of this age, and were unable to engage in productive, meaningful activity. Their intellectual operations thus remained very limited; even such operations as elementary classification were beyond them.

In order to discover the factors that played a leading role in the development of speech and the changes that might be brought about in the construction of the twins' mental life as a result of the rapid acquisition of language, we undertook a special experiment.

It was necessary, to ensure a rapid development of speech, to create an objective necessity for using language in the company of speaking children. We therefore removed the 'twin situation' by separating the children and placing them in separate, parallel groups in a kindergarten and then observed the changes that took place in their speech. Subsequently we conducted a special systematic experiment in teaching speech with one of the twins, with the aim of developing perception of speech, the habit of making use of developed sentences etc.

Our experiment produced very rapid results.

As a result of removal of the 'twin situation' primitive speech, interlocked with practical activity, very quickly fell into the background and in the new situation the children were soon in a position to pass on to communicating with the aid of a normal language system.

Three months after the experiment began we could already observe substantial improvements in the twins' speech. Leaving aside small phonetic defects, the lexicology and grammar of their speech approximated to the normal speech of their counterparts. Their speech also fulfilled new functions which had formerly been absent; in place of speech interlocked with direct activity, or expressive speech, there developed narrative and then planning speech.

Even more significant was the fact that the whole structure of the mental life of both twins was simultaneously and sharply changed. Once they acquired an objective language system, the children were able to formulate the aims of their activity verbally and after only three months we observed the beginnings of meaningful play; there arose the possibility of productive, constructive activity in the light of formulated aims, and to an important degree there were separated out a series of intellectual operations which shortly before this were only in an embryonic state.

In the course of further observations we were able to note cardinal improvements in the structure of the twins' mental life which we could only attribute to the influence of the one changed factor – the acquisition of a language system. Differences between the children also arose connected with the systematic training of Twin A in customary speech; he was thereby enabled to make speech an object of perception and to develop grammatically developed forms of speech communication. Our records showed that this was reflected in specific speech operations and discursive thinking in the case of this twin, in which he perceptibly surpassed the other.

Therefore the results of our experiment show that, with the creation of an objective necessity for speech communication, the children were satisfactorily prepared for the acquisition of a language system; not only did they develop new forms of communication with the aid of developing verbal speech, but also there were called forth significant changes in the structure of their conscious activity, built up on the basis of verbal speech.

There is no doubt that these facts provide new material for an understanding of the changes brought about by speech in the formation of the more complex mental processes in man.

Notes

1. A basic conception of the child's mental development has been set out in detail by L. S. Vigotsky, *The Intellectual Development of Children in the Process of Education* (Moscow, 1935).

2. This proposition has been developed in the work of A. N. Leontiev, see 'The nature and formation of mental properties and processes in man', *Questions of Psychology*, no. 1, 1955. Translated in *Psychology in the Soviet Union*, ed. Brian Simon (1956, p. 226 ff.).

3. I. P. Pavlov, *Collected Works*, vol. 3 (Moscow, 1949; see *Selected Works*, Moscow, 1955, p. 537); an English translation published by the Foreign Languages Publishing House.

4. L. S. Vigotsky, *Thought and Language*, Harfmann & Vaker, MIT Press, 1962.

5. A. N. Leontiev, *The Development of Memory* (Moscow, 1930).

6. G. L. Rosengardt-Pupko, *Speech and the Development of the Child's Perception* (Moscow, 1947). F. I. Fradkina, 'The rise of the child's speech', *Scientific Notes of the Leningrad Educational Institute*, vol. 7, 1955; T. E. Konnikova, 'The first stage in the development of the child's speech', *Thesis*, A. I. Herzen's Educational Institute, Leningrad (1947); E. K. Kaverina, *The Development of Children's Speech during the First Two Years of Life* (Moscow, 1950); M. M. Koltsova, 'The rise and development of the second signal system in the child', *Researches of the Laboratories of I. P. Pavlov*, vol. 4, 1949; 'Studies in the formation of the signal systems in the child', *Thesis*, Institute of Physiology, Academy of Sciences of the USSR, Leningrad (1953).

7. The work of A. N. Leontiev and A. V. Zaporozhets and the closely connected work of D. B. Elkonin, N. G. Morozov, L. S. Slavina and others. See *Questions of Child Psychology*, ed. A. N. Leontiev, *Proceedings of the Academy of Educational Sciences of the RSFSR* vol. 14, 1948.

8. A. G. Ivanov-Smolensky, 'Concerning the study of the joint activity of the first and second signal systems', *Journal of Higher Nervous Activity*, vol. 1, no. 1, 1951; 'The interaction of the first and second signal systems in certain normal and pathological conditions', *Physiological Journal of the USSR* vol. 35, no. 5, 1949. N. I. Krasnogorsky, *Studies of Higher Nervous Activity in Animals and in Man*, vol. I (Moscow, 1954).

9. M. S. Bychkov, L. A. Shvarts and others.

10. 'The role of the word in the development of the child's cognitive activity', *Speeches at the Conference on Psychological Questions, July 1953* (Moscow, 1954). Translated in *Psychology in the Soviet Union*, p. 197 ff. In her later work Lublinskaya has disclosed changes introduced by the word into the process of forming images, 'Certain peculiarities in the interaction of speech and image in the pre-school child', *Questions of Psychology*, no. 1, 1956.

11. L. I. Kotliarevsky and V. K. Fadeeva have shown that this takes place in children.

12. E. N. Martsinovskaya, 'An investigation of the reflectory and regulating role of the second signal system in children of pre-school age', *Proceedings of the Department of Psychology, Moscow University*; L. A. Abramian, 'Organization of the child's voluntary activity with the aid of verbal instruction', *Thesis*, Moscow University (1955).

13. L. S. Vigotsky and A. R. Luria, 'The function and fate of ego-centric speech', *Proceedings of the Ninth International Psychological Congress* (New Haven, 1929).

14. N. P. Paramonova, 'Development of the interaction of the two signal systems in the formation of motor reactions in children of pre-school age', *Thesis*, Moscow University (1953).

15. And the closely related research of G. A. Kisliuk.

16. A. I. Meshcheriakov, 'Disturbance of the interaction of the two signal systems in the formation of simple motor reactions in cases of local paralysis of the brain', *Thesis*, Moscow University (1953). M. P. Ivanova, 'Disturbance of the interaction of the two signal systems in the formation of complex motor reactions in cases of paralysis of the brain', *Thesis*, Moscow University (1953). V. I. Lubovsky, 'Some peculiarities of the joint work of the two signal systems in the formation of motor reactions in oligophrenic children', *Thesis*, Moscow University (1955). E. N. Martinovskaya, 'Disturbance of the generalizing function of speech in the formation of temporary connections in mentally retarded children', *Thesis*, Moscow University (1953).

17. Some light is thrown on these questions in a paper by A. R. Luria, 'The role of language in the formation of temporary connections in man', *Questions of Psychology*, no. 1, 1955. Translated in *Psychology in the Soviet Union*, p. 115 ff.

18. A. Gelb and K. Goldstein, *A Psychological Analysis of Neuropathological Cases* (Leipzig, 1920); K. Goldstein, *The Construction of the Organism* (The Hague, 1934); A. Gelb, Medical psychology, *Acta Psychologica*, 1937; H. Head, *Aphasia and Kindred Diseases of Speech*, vols. 1 and 2 (Oxford, 1926).

19. R. M. Boskis, *The Development of Verbal Speech in the Deaf-Mute Child* (Moscow, 1939); N. G. Morozova, *The Teaching of Conscious Reading to Deaf-Mute Schoolchildren* (Moscow, 1953); B. D. Korsunskaya and N. G. Morozova, *Producing Concepts in the First Classes of Deaf-Mute Schools* (Moscow, 1939).

20. See A. N. Sokolov, 'Speech mechanisms of intellectual activity', *Proceedings of the Academy of Educational Sciences of the RSFSR*, vol. 81, 1956; N. I. Zhinkin, *The Mechanisms of Speech* (Moscow, 1958), L. K. Nazarova, 'The role of speech kinesthesis in writing', *Soviet Education*, no. 6, 1952.

21. An exceptional case, studied by A. R. Luria, was a patient with weakened speech kinesthesis whose speech processes flowed only in the form of external speech so that the simple pressing down of the tongue led to almost complete exclusion of speech from the flow of complex mental processes.

22. N. P. Paramonova (1953); A. A. Lublinskaya (1953; 1956).

23. These tests are discussed in A. R. Luria, *Traumatic Aphasia* (Moscow, 1947).

24. Following the method worked out by A. N. Mirenova; see A. R. Luria, 'The development of constructive activity in the pre-school child', in *Psychology of the Pre-School Child*, ed. A. N. Leontiev and A. V. Zaporozhets (Moscow, 1948).

25. A. R. Luria, 'Defects in grammatical operations in cases of brain disease', *Proceedings of the Academy of Educational Sciences of the RSFSR*, vol. 3 (1946). The subject has recently been dealt with by S. N. Karpova, 'Perception of the verbal structure of speech', *Questions of Psychology*, no. 4, 1955.

Other Penguin Papers in Education

Young Teachers and Reluctant Learners

An account of the Hillview project, an experiment in teacher
education, and a discussion of its educational implications

Charles Hannam, Pat Smyth and Norman Stephenson

No teacher in secondary schools can avoid having to cope with
'difficult' adolescents or 'reluctant learners' (or whatever the
preferred euphemism might be). With the imminent raising of the
school-leaving age such problems are bound to be intensified. There
are obviously no easy answers, but essential to any kind of progress
is a more detailed and sympathetic insight into the out-of-school
lives of these children, a more sensitive awareness of who they are.

This book discusses some of the problems in relations between teachers
and pupils – problems which, though real, are often unacknowledged.
The Hillview project in the Bristol University School of Education
took trainee teachers directly into the out-of-school lives of
'difficult' fifteen year olds over the period of a year. This account of
the experiment draws on the journals kept by the students, and includes
many tape-recorded extracts of conversations with the teenagers they
worked with.

But the book is much more than an account of a teacher-training
project. It suggests many fresh insights into the issues of social class,
authority, language and attitudes in relation to reluctant learners.
Both the nature of these children and the problems which all teachers
have to face become clearer, more manageable, more human.

Language, the Learner and the School
Revised edition

A Research Report by Douglas Barnes with a contribution from
James Britton and a Discussion Document prepared by Harold Rosen
on behalf of the London Association for the Teaching of English

Douglas Barnes, James Britton, Harold Rosen and the L.A.T.E.

Language is the most subtle and pervasive of the means by which
we present our assumptions about role, about subject-matter, and
about the people we talk to, at and with. And yet, as Douglas Barnes's
fascinating survey of secondary-school classrooms shows, teachers
tend to talk too much (and pupils too little) and are often also
insensitive to the effects and significance of the language they
use and expect. What can we learn about learning by looking at the
language of our classrooms?

Douglas Barnes's research was aimed at finding some answers to this
important question. James Britton's contribution switches attention
to the pupil: what function does talk have – even ordinary,
undemanding, trivial talk for talk's sake – in the development of
thought. This revised edition contains a new version of the
'discussion document', designed to bring together teachers of all
subjects in a common 'language policy' within the school, and an
account by Harold Rosen of the work going on in schools directly
instigated by the first edition of this book.